WITTGENSTEIN'S DOCTRINE OF THE
TYRANNY OF LANGUAGE

WITTGENSTEIN'S DOCTRINE OF THE TYRANNY OF LANGUAGE

AN HISTORICAL AND CRITICAL EXAMINATION OF HIS BLUE BOOK

by

S. MORRIS ENGEL

University of Southern California

WITH AN INTRODUCTION
BY
STEPHEN TOULMIN

MARTINUS NIJHOFF / THE HAGUE / 1975

PHOTOMECHANICAL REPRINT

ISBN 90 247 1185 1

PRINTED IN THE NETHERLANDS

To The Memory Of
My Mother
FEIGE LEAH ENGEL

TABLE OF CONTENTS

INTRODUCTION

Stephen Toulmin

George Santayana used to insist that those who are ignorant of the history of thought are doomed to re-enact it. To this we can add a corollary: that those who are ignorant of the context of ideas are doomed to misunderstand them. In a few self-contained fields such as pure mathematics, concepts and conceptual systems can perhaps be detached from their historico-cultural situations; so that (for instance) a self-taught Ramanujan, living alone in India, mastered number-theory to a point at which he could make major contributions to European mathematics. But elsewhere the situation is different – and, in philosophy, inevitably so. For philosophical ideas and problems confront us like geological specimens *in situ*; and, in the act of prising them free from their historical and cultural locations, we can too easily forget about the matrix in which they took shape, and end by impossing on them a sculptural form of our own making.

Something of this kind has happened in the case of Ludwig Wittgenstein. For his philosophical work has commonly been seen as an episode in the development, either of mathematical logic, or of twentieth-century British philosophy. His associations with Frege and Russell, Moore and Waismann, have over-shadowed everything else in his cultural origins and intellectual concerns. As a result, he has been applauded or attacked as the co-author of the method of truth-tables, as a dominant influence on the positivism of the 1920s and 30s, as a critic of private languages and sense-data, as the analyst of intellectual cramps and language-games – in short, as the man who took the ideas and methods of Moore and Russell's "analytical revolution" in philosophy, and refined them far beyond anything their first authors had imagined. Not surprisingly, that is how Moore and Russell themselves saw him. To Russell, Wittgenstein was the young engineering apprentice at Metro-

politan Vickers who sent him queries about *Principia Mathematica* and
subsequently became his own most talented graduate student. And
Moore's attitude is well expressed in the examiner's report which he is
apocryphally reported to have submitted, when Wittgenstein presented
the *Tractatus Logico-Philosophicus* as his doctoral dissertation:

> It is my personal opinion that Mr Wittgenstein's thesis is a work
> of genius. But, be that as it may, it is certainly well up to the
> standard required for the Cambridge degree of Doctor of Philo-
> sophy.

If we look at Wittgenstein only from this English standpoint, however,
we shall end by misunderstanding many features of his life and work:
his philosophical aims and methods, even the very nature of his results.
This danger is only enhanced if we think of him, as Moore evidently did,
as someone extraordinary, phenomenal, even unique. For, as we are
now at last beginning to see, *uniqueness* is the one thing Wittgenstein
cannot – as a philosopher – claim. Far from being an English-language
philosopher with an unprecedented genius and an unparalleled point of
view, Wittgenstein was an absolutely first-rate Viennese thinker, whose
achievements summed up – even epitomised – the intellectual preoccupations of his native milieu.

Let me here interject a personal remark, addressed primarily to my
own former self: that is, to the young physics student who first attended
Wittgenstein's classes in that sparsely furnished eagle's-nest of a room,
at the top of the tower in Whewell's Court at Trinity College, Cambridge, some thirty years ago. Certainly, at the time, we who heard
Wittgenstein lecture found his ideas, his methods of argument, even his
very topics of discussion, completely original; and the same was still
true, five years later, of those who attended his final year's classes in
1946–47. Seen against an English background, Wittgenstein's later
work appeared as unique and extraordinary as the *Tractatus* had
appeared to Moore. Meanwhile, for our own part, we struck Wittgenstein as intolerably stupid, and he was sometimes in despair about
getting us to grasp what he was talking about. At the time, this mutual
incomprehension seemed to us an inevitable outcome of the unique and
unparalleled character of Wittgenstein's approach: with commendable
modesty, we strove only the harder to master the mysteries involved.
Looking back from the present time, however, I would now put it down
to a culture-clash: the clash between a Viennese thinker whose whole
mind had been formed in a post-Kantian environment, and an audience

of students who came to him with attitudes and preoccupations shaped by the neo-Humean (and so, implicitly, pre-Kantian) empiricism of Moore, Russell and their associates.

At the time, Wittgenstein might seem to have been spinning the whole substance of his later philosophy out of his own head, like some intellectually creative spider. Yet, in fact, much of his material had origins which we in Britain knew next-to-nothing about; while he concentrated on problems many of which had been in the centre of discussion among German-speaking philosophers and psychologists since before the First World War. As to the material: Wittgenstein himself credited the best-known of his ambiguous figures (the "duck-rabbit") to its author, Jastrow. Other of his characteristic illustrations came from the *Gestalt* psychologists, notably from Koffka. Meanwhile, the sources of others again are only now coming to light. Professor Robert Fogelin of Yale has pointed out to me, for instance, that so crucial a notion as that of "forms of life" or *Lebensformen* – of which Wittgenstein says, in the *Philosophical Investigations*:

> What has to be accepted, the given, is – so one could say – *forms of life*

– itself has important connections in the Vienna of Wittgenstein's own time. Among the most successful works of popular neo-Kantian literature after the First World War was an essay in "characterology" by Eduard Spranger, which had sold by the late 1920s (I find) as many as 28,000 copies; and the very title of this book was *Lebensformen*! Given his Viennese background, Wittgenstein was thus in no more position to invent the phrase "forms of life" than I would myself be today to invent the phrase "territorial imperative."

But it is not only in his examples, and his terminology, that Wittgenstein was indebted to his Viennese contemporaries and forerunners. His central philosophical preoccupations, too, are intelligible (I would argue) only against a Kantian backcloth. Like Kant and Schopenhauer before him, Wittgenstein was essentially preoccupied with the notions of intellectual "bounds" or "limits," and with the impulse of the human mind to transcend them. In his arguments Kant's fundamental questions about the scope and limits of the reason (*Vernunft*), which had been transformed by Schopenhauer into questions about the scope and limits of representation (*Vorstellung*), were converted once again into questions about the scope and limits of language (*Sprache*). In private conversations with Waismann, Wittgenstein talked about these limits

(*Grenze*) and about the human impulse to over-run them (*an die Grenze der Sprache anzurennen*), in terms which he explicitly compared with Kierkegaard and Heidegger, and which have clear affiliations with the whole tradition of "critical" or "transcendental" analysis founded by Kant, and continued throughout all subsequent German philosophy. In the *Tractatus*, Wittgenstein evidently believed that the scope and limits of language – which were also the scope and limits of the intellect, or of thought – could be mapped definitively by applying the techniques and symbolism of Russell's propositional calculus. As the 1920s went on – and especially after 1927, when he began regular discussions with Schlick and Waismann – he gradually lost this confidence. Whereas he had earlier taken for granted the existence of some direct *Verbindung der Sprache und der Wirklichkeit*, he now acknowledged that some more explicit account was required of the relations between language and the world.

The full significance of this Kantian background to our view of Wittgenstein and his philosophical ideas will take some time to work out. So many of his later colleagues and associates came to philosophy from an English-language background that hardly any of them have appreciated hitherto the nature of Wittgenstein's debts to his German-speaking origins and upbringing.

Professor Engel here makes a highly useful contribution to the task which now faces us, of putting Wittgenstein back into his original context, and recognizing the problems he was concerned with as a philosopher throughout his career. The picture of Wittgenstein as the creature of Moore and Russell runs up against one fatal obstacle: Wittgenstein himself sought out Frege in the first place, and he did so, evidently, with some well-formed philosophical questions in mind. In order to reconstruct these questions, we must consider the nature of Wittgenstein's training as a physicist, and his consequent debt to Heinrich Hertz – a task to be undertaken elsewhere, and by others – but we must also place Wittgenstein in a philosophical perspective that relates his work to Mauthner's *Sprachkritik*, to Schopenhauer's *Fourfold Root*, to Kierkegaard – whose ethical position Wittgenstein largely shared – to Kant, to Lichtenberg – from whom he took the term "paradigm" – and to many others whose books were universal reading in the literary and educated Vienna of Wittgenstein's youth.

"Well started is half done." In this book, Professor Engel claims only to be opening up some of the questions which we shall all be having to pursue further in the years ahead. This is a modest claim, which he entirely fulfills. He has many highly suggestive things to say, and he draws many highly significant parallels between the problems and arguments of Ludwig Wittgenstein and those of earlier philosophers in the same critical and transcendental tradition. Far from presenting his own methods of philosophising as involving a complete break with the past, Wittgenstein himself used to speak of philosophy – as he did it – as being "the legitimate heir to what has hitherto been called 'philosophy'." We shall understand fully the force of this description, only when we put Wittgenstein back into the great tradition of historical philosophers who have tried to work their way beyond the point at which Hume (and his latter-day revivers) left the subject, and to give some satisfactory account of the manner in which reason, representation, language, concept-acquisition – call it what you will – plays an indispensable part in the definition of thought and experience. In this respect, Professor Engel does us a real service, when he calls on us to see Wittgenstein's work, not as the repudiation of our philosophical tradition, but rather as its proper twentieth-century continuation.

PREFACE

This little book grows out of an attempt to understand how some philosophers within the linguistic movement have come to say the very strange things now so familiar to us. Having for a very long time been both puzzled and intrigued by them I finally determined to discover what some of their origins were and what about them was so puzzling and intriguing to me. Although I very soon discovered these origins in Wittgenstein's *Blue Book*, the tensions and contradictions which I found in this work, as well as Wittgenstein's differences with his disciples, proved to be themselves very puzzling and I set about to trace their roots as well. The result is the work which the reader has before him.

It begins by describing how philosophy and the motives which are thought to give rise to it have come to be viewed in our time by some philosophers. It then shows how the two strands in this view represent two different aspects of Wittgenstein's *Blue Book*, each reflecting, in turn, two diverse literary sources and traditions. Although both would seem to be necessary in order to make a convincing case for the position argued, they are insufficiently harmonized in Wittgenstein and not at all or only superficially in the work of others to successfully accomplish this. What these aspects are, how they have come to be responsible for the strains and stresses of the *Blue Book*, and how and what about this strange book has proven to be so misleading, is the theme of this study.

Although it is an author's privilege to choose the theme he wishes to deal with and limit his study to it, the reader may nevertheless find the present choice surprising and wonder why so much attention should be given to the *Blue Book* when we now have and have had for some years the far more substantial *Philosophical Investigations*. It is my hope, however, that after reading this study he will come to agree that the *Blue Book* is a work of great philosophical and historical interest in its own right and can hardly be neglected in any attempt to understand either the development of Wittgenstein's thought or some of our recent philosophical tendencies. On the other hand, the reason for neglecting the *Philosophical Investigations* here is due to the fact, of course, that that work became available only when the philosophical tendencies under examination here were already well in motion, and what set them in motion was not the *Philosophical Investigations* but the *Blue Book*. Although, therefore, the *Philosophical Investigations* is briefly discussed toward the end of this study, it is not relevant to its early portions. The same applies, accordingly, to those historical influences and parallels traced here. Only those influences and parallels directly relevant to my theme have been brought to bear upon it. Those more directly relevant to themes more substantially developed or found only in the *Philosophical Investigations* have generally been omitted from this account.

Regarding these influences, whose discovery perhaps may make some readers somewhat uneasy, I should like to say that in tracing them it has not been my intention to lay more stress upon them than they deserve. Certainly it has not been my intention to try to show how, for example, Kant or Spinoza or Schopenhauer "anticipated" Wittgenstein. Like the tracing of "influences" so popular in an older age of scholarship there is something dissatisfying and inconsequential about this kind of enterprise. For it is not what one writer owes to, or has borrowed from another that is really of any great interest; rather, it is what he has done with it and the new kind of life he has breathed into it that is of interest to us. And from this point of view there can be no doubt that Wittgenstein has added, as we say, a new dimension to the thought and ideas of these thinkers and expressed their insights in a new and striking idiom, one which, unlike perhaps its old terminology, is alive with meaning for us. For what becomes obsolete in a philosophical treatise, it seems to me, is not (unlike the case with a scientific treatise) its content, but only its language or expression. But since its very life depends upon that expression, to give a philosophical idea a new expression is in a very real sense to rediscover it.

That this procedure contains various dangers is obvious from Wittgenstein's own example, whose clinical and lexical language – some of the historical origins of which I have tried to trace here – has led some to desert philosophy for psychoanalysis (as seems to have happened, for example, with Lazerowitz) and others to desert philosophy for lexicography (which is what a good deal of recent work in the linguistic movement amounts to).

A new terminology, however, brings along with it possibilities of new understanding. It helps uncover old truths by focusing upon facets of a discipline which the old terminology obscures or hides from us. It need not be a matter of trying to bring the insights of one discipline to bear upon another and thus, as has sometimes been suggested, to do violence to both. Nothing of the sort need ever result from such a confrontation, as Wittgenstein's example also makes obvious. For who can fail to see that by showing in the new and striking way that he does how certain of our statements refer only to themselves and how puzzlement arises from confusing the grammatical with the experiential, he once again has enabled us to come to terms with those insights of Spinoza and Kant expressed by them in such well-known but now esoteric doctrines as, for example, that all explanations are mere modes of imagining and do not indicate the true nature of anything, and, by Kant, in the view that metaphysical questions arise from our attempt to apply and extend the categories to an area where they do not apply?

Such connections between the works of Wittgenstein and those of Spinoza, Kant, Schopenhauer, etc. do, however, exist. The tendency thus far has been to ignore them or even to deny them. After reading this book I hope the reader will see that this has been a mistake. For such sources and parallels throw a good deal of light upon Wittgenstein's philosophy; they do not in any way detract from its importance and originality. On the contrary, by placing him within the tradition, as I have tried to do here, his works take on new meaning and gain in stature. Ultimately this is what I have hoped to achieve here. Aware as I am, however, of all the pitfalls which lie in the path of anyone setting out to explain an author to both his friends and foes, I do not pride myself on having achieved it. It is my hope, however, that this book will make it easier for others to do so.

Los Angeles, California
March, 1968.

Every great truth before its discovery is announced
by a previous feeling, a presentiment, a faint outline
as in fog, and an unavailing attempt to grasp it;
simply because the progress of the time has prepared it. It is, therefore, preceded by disjointed
utterances. But he alone, who has recognized a
truth from its causes, and thought it out to its consequences, developed its whole content, cast his
eyes over the extent of its domain, and after this,
with a full consciousness of its value and importance,
clearly and connectedly expounded it, he alone is
its originator.

Schopenhauer ("History of Philosophy")

CHAPTER ONE

A PAGE IN RECENT PHILOSOPHICAL HISTORY

I

Of all the books which have been written in the past ten years or so regarding the so-called "revolution" in philosophy, none perhaps have been as widely read and acclaimed as Mr. Warnock's *English Philosophy Since 1900*.[1] It has become something of a classic.

Written, however, before the publication of Wittgenstein's *Blue and Brown Books*, its account of Wittgenstein's place and role in this history is not entirely satisfactory, missing completely as it does a certain tendency in that history which derives from a side of Wittgenstein Mr. Warnock could not completely gather from the *Tractatus* or the *Investigations* which are his primary texts.

Still no one, it seems to me, has described better the background and setting of this revolution (and especially G. E. Moore's role in it) than Mr. Warnock. Before going on to describe the part he has missed, I will let him tell that part of it which he has described so well.

Readers of Nietzsche will remember his striking thesis that it was Socrates, the opponent of Dionysus, who destroyed Greek tragedy. Unlike his predecessors among the spectators, so runs Nietzsche's famous thesis, Socrates no longer understood the language of tragedy and asked that it be made clear to him what it was that was asserted on stage. It was a preposterous request, says Nietzsche, but Greek tragedy was wrecked on it.

Mr. Warnock does not mention this historical precedent nor does he draw this parallel, but what he says about the death of British Idealism bears a striking resemblance to it.

British Idealism, he says, perished at the hands of G. E. Moore. But it was not, he goes on to explain, "by reason of his intellectual gifts," (p. 12) nor by refutation, that this was accomplished. Metaphysical

---

[1] (London: Oxford University Press, 1958).

systems, he observes, do not as a rule yield to "frontal attack." "Their odd property of being demonstrable only, so to speak, from within confers on them also a high resistance to attack from outside." It is rather from neglect that such systems finally perish. "They are citadels," he says, "which are quietly discovered one day to be no longer inhabited." With Absolute Idealism, "the old spells were broken, and a new spell was cast" chiefly, he suggests, by reason of the *character* of G. E. Moore.[2]

What was it about Moore's character which led to this disastrous result?

In the first place, he seems to have been, Mr. Warnock explains, "entirely without any of the motives that tend to make a metaphysician." (p. 12)

He was neither discontented with nor puzzled by the ordinary beliefs of plain men and plain scientists. He had no leanings whatever towards paradox and peculiarity of opinion. He had no particular religious or other cosmic anxieties; and he seems to have felt that in aesthetics and morality (not, of course, in moral or aesthetic *philosophy*) all was as well, at least, as could reasonably be expected. (P. 12)

"The character of his original interest in philosophy was," Mr. Warnock goes on to relate, "both very simple and, in its context, strikingly original." (p. 13)

He went to Cambridge in 1892 to read classics, hardly aware at that time "that there was such a subject as philosophy." But the encouragement of, among others, Bertrand Russell first engaged his interest in philosophical discussions, and then led him, at the end of his first year, to start reading philosophy. His concern with the subject was, in a sense, indirect. "I do not think that the world or the sciences would ever have suggested to me any philosophical problems. What has suggested philosophical problems to me is things which other philosophers have said about the world or the sciences." In discussions at Cambridge he heard propositions asserted to which he could attach no clear meaning, and he sought to have it explained what their meaning was. He heard things asserted which he could see no sufficient reason to believe, and he tried to find out on what grounds the assertions were made. It appeared to him that his companions sometimes denied what every sane man knew quite well to be true, and he made patient efforts to persuade them that they ought not to do this. (p. 13–4)

"The most striking feature of his philosophical questioning was," Mr. Warnock continues, "its very simplicity and directness." (p. 14)

---

[2] P. 11. In saying this Mr. Warnock does not mean to imply, of course, that it was Moore's *personality* which had this effect upon his contemporaries. By Moore's "character" he means, rather, Moore's way of doing philosophy, the peculiar spirit which infected his arguments, the simplicity and naivete displayed in them, and so on.

His mind ... always worked most naturally in concrete terms. If Time is unreal, ought we not to deny that we have breakfast *before* we have lunch? ... Moore did not in every case wish to suggest that the strange things philosophers said were certainly untrue. But he did wish to make it quite plain that they were very strange. He wished to point out how astonishing were their implications. ... In all of this he was neither obstinate not disingenuous ... His puzzlement, indeed his bewilderment, at the things they were willing to assert was entirely sincere. (Pp. 14–5)

For example:

It was supposedly agreed on all hands that quite ordinary opinions were quite certainly defective; that common ways of speaking were almost always unsatisfactory; and that *therefore* it was quite clearly imperative to devise new ways of speaking, new and subtler opinions, in order to withstand the close scrutiny of philosophical criticism. Moore ... asked ... what exactly was supposed to be wrong with very ordinary opinions? Why exactly were common ways of speaking to be condemned? So far from being disposed to assume that beliefs very widely held were very probably mistaken, he was inclined to suppose that they were almost certain to be true. ... For some people at least, the mere raising of such questions as these – the mere refusal to submit without question to Idealist spells – had apparently the force of a liberation. ... Why should one try to believe that Time is not real? There was quite suddenly seen to be no reason at all. (Pp. 16–7)

This is, as everyone will recognize, an admirable portrait of Moore. It not only illuminates Moore's own philosophical writings (including the peculiar fascination which they have had upon so many) but it also, what is of immediate interest to us here, throws a great deal of light on the philosophising of those who now followed in Moore's footsteps. For the naivete, real or assumed, which characterizes so much of their work can be traced directly to this impact and influence which Moore had on them. And in this sense Mr. Warnock is no doubt right in stressing that it was not so much Moore's thought as his character which affected so profoundly the thinking of those who fell under his spell. Profound changes of this kind border on conversion and are rarely the product of calm deliberation.

But although Moore must be credited for being the first (at least in recent times) to ask why philosophers were led to say such strangely curious things, he did not himself bother to pursue it. He never had, as Mr. Warnock further points out in his book, a general answer as to why philosophers held opinions or asserted doctrines which were seemingly incompatible with what they themselves and others knew to be true. He was satisfied in merely being able to point out that this was unhappily so.

But once raised, of course, its exploration was inevitably and others quickly undertook to carry it out.

Nor had they, as it turned out, very far to seek for the solution to this problem which now began more and more to fascinate them. Various theories regarding the nature of philosophic activity which were at that very moment being propounded seemed to be just the sort of thing which was wanted. Moore's attack and the character of his approach made these writers extremely receptive to these doctrines, and they quickly fell under their spell.

But I should like to leave Mr. Warnock's account at this point, for I am not, like he, interested in tracing the several different answers given by several different philosophers to this question raised by Moore, but wish rather to trace instead the effect which *Wittgenstein's* answer to it had upon the thinking of those who fell under *his* spell. For there were two separate wings to his answer and although Mr. Warnock (as I have already pointed out) certainly does justice to one of these wings, the other is not dealt with at all by him. But this is not surprising, for these two separate wings are not as easily identifiable in the *Blue Book* as they are in those who took their inspiration from it and tended to separate into these two different camps.

I should like, therefore, to skip over not only such contributions to this question as were made by such philosophers as, for example, Bertrand Russell and Gilbert Ryle (whose views Mr. Warnock discusses in detail) but also (for the moment) such answers as were given by Wittgenstein himself, and turn instead to the interpretation placed upon those answers by those who found them irresistible.

Now Ayer was, perhaps, one of the first to do so and to become representative of one of those two trends I want to briefly sketch here.

In an article published in 1934 and entitled "The Genesis of Metaphysics," he offered the following notorious diagnosis. "The best example I can give," he remarked, "of the way in which metaphysics normally comes to be written is a passage from Heidegger's "Was ist Metaphysik."[3]

"Only Being," says Heidegger, "ought to be explored and besides that – nothing: Being alone and further – nothing: Being solely and beyond that – nothing. How about this nothing? Is there the nothing only because there is the not – that is

---

[3] *Analysis*, Vol. 1, No. 4; reprinted in *Philosophy and Analysis*, ed. Margaret Macdonald (New York: Philosophical Library, 1954). The example itself Ayer found, as he himself tells us, in Carnap. As a result of this attention it is now probably the most famous single passage in all of Heidegger.

Negation? Or is it the other way about? Is there Negation and the not only because there is the nothing? We assert: the nothing is more fundamental than the not and Negation. Where are we to look for the nothing? How are we to find the nothing? We know the nothing. Anxiety (Die Angst) reveals the nothing. That for which and about which we made ourselves anxious was "really" nothing. In fact the nothing itself, as such, was there. How does this nothing? The Nothing nothings itself. (Das Nichts selbst nichtet)." (Pp. 23–4)

"This passage," Ayer went on to suggest, "is important not merely because it shows the psychologist what down right nonsense a philosopher, accounted eminent, will in all innocence produce, but even more because it exemplifies so very clearly the kind of error which lies at the root of almost all metaphysics." (p. 24)

For what sustains this rubbish is the single false assumption that the sentences "there is snow on the ground" and "there is nothing on the ground" express propositions of the same logical form. It is this that leads the author to enquire into the state of the nothing, just as he might ask about the state of the snow, and finally to the introduction of the nonsense verb to nothing by analogy with the verb to snow. The fallacy is one which readers of Lewis Carroll will enjoy to recognise. "I am sure nobody walks much faster than I do." "He can't do that," said the king, "or else he'd have been here first."[4]

This, Ayer claimed, was the explanation of the notorious difficulties which students have always experienced with the writings of metaphysicians. It has simply been the inherent deceptions of language – its built-in ambiguities, its misleading forms (so similar in appearance but yet so different, often, in their logical import) – which has proven so fatal to philosophers. Had Heidegger been more attentive he would not have gone on to posit (of all things) the existence of Nothing and to say how it *nothings* itself!

There is no need to point out here the source of these new theories which Ayer was beginning to make use of in his attempt to answer the question Moore posed. That is now well-known. But what is perhaps interesting to note at this point is that as incredible as this piece of analysis of the "error" he thought Heidegger had made may now appear to us, it was not even then, now that we can look back on it, so entirely new. G. E. Moore himself, as early as 1903, had, without really knowing it, stumbled upon something very similar in, of all places, Mill. Quoting Mill's now famous statement:

---

[4] *Ibid.* Ayer's own philosophical outlook is, of course, a good deal more complicated than is implied by this simple reference and his philosophical debts a good deal more various. I am here, however, interested in isolating only those factors and stages of recent philosophical history that are immediately relevant to my theme.

The only proof capable of being given that a thing is visible, is that people actually see it. The only proof that a sound is audible, is that people hear it; and so of
the other sources of our experience. In like manner, I apprehend, the sole evidence
it is possible to produce that anything is desirable, is that people actually desire it.

– he went on to point out (very much in the way Ayer was later to) how
Mill had fallen victim here to a truly striking deception. "The fallacy
... is so obvious," he declared (perhaps not quite believing it himself),
"that it is quite wonderful how Mill failed to see it. The fact is that
'desirable' does not mean 'able to be desired' as 'visible' means 'able to
be seen.' The desirable means simply what *ought* to be desired or
deserves to be desired."[5] What Mill had done was to confuse "the
proper sense of 'desirable' in which it denotes that which it is good to
desire, with the sense which it would bear if it were analogous to such
words as 'visible'." (p. 67) And, of course, it is not so analogous.

Now although that was certainly an interesting observation and even
perhaps something of an anticipation of what was to come, it was for
Moore in 1903, we should perhaps add, really not much more than that,
he certainly did not try, as others were to later, to build a whole *theory*
around it. For him it was simply an isolated observation of an amusing
curiosity. Furthermore, and this again indicates how far he was from
having a full-blown theory about it, Moore did not say explicitly, although he seems on the verge of doing so, that it was the "uniform
appearances" of the words "desirable," "visible" and "audible" which
led Mill to confuse them. For him, Mill, apparently, had simply confused them because of his momentary inattentiveness to their divergent
meanings. And that of course is not the same as having a theory about
such things.

The way such confusions, however, came to be regarded by the time
of Ayer's paper was something else entirely. On the contrary, people
now saw such confusions as somehow arising from language itself and
as intimately bound up with it. Such confusions were not now regarded,
that is to say, as mere accidents, or momentary, inexplicable lapses.
Such lapses, it was now maintained, had causes and, in a way, were
even inevitable – especially where philosophers were concerned. And
that was the important new discovery people like Ayer now believed
had been made. This discovery was to be explored, as the literature of
the period indicates, in all sorts of new and interesting ways and often
even with great subtlety and ingenuity. But even in such sophisticated
analysis as that of the Free-Will Problem where it was shown how the

[5] *Principia Ethica* (Cambridge: At the University Press, 1959), p. 67.

confusion of "freedom" with "indeterminism," and of "compulsion" with "determinism" resulted in the drawing of false contrasts and parallels which in turn generated the whole problem, that main point, that somehow the trouble lay in language itself, was never lost sight of.

But so much for this *linguistic* strain in recent analytic philosophy.

2

If some analysts, however, believed this account of the origin of philosophical nonsense, there were also some (forming a rather different wing of recent analytic philosophy) who were beginning to have their doubts. The linguistic diagnosis began to look to them as somehow too simple, too incredible, too absurd. It seemed to lack depth, necessity and inevitableness. If language truly doomed metaphysicians to speak nonsense, the doom, their instincts told them, must be sealed at a level deeper than the strictly linguistic one. Drawing heavily, like the others, from Wittgenstein, they argued that what doomed philosophers to speak nonsense was something deeply psychological. This manifests itself in language and can be approached in this manner, but it was not something strictly or simply linguistic. An extreme representative of this *clinical* wing, as I shall call it, of the analytic movement is Lazerowitz.

What is to be made of such sentences as "Anxiety reveals the nothing," "We know the nothing," "The nothing exists," Lazerowitz asked? "What sort of mistake, if any," he enquired, "is a person making who utters them?"[6] Although certainly absurd, may they not, perhaps, have an interesting content to them?

Returning to what Moore had said, Lazerowitz admitted that there was indeed something very paradoxical about metaphysical statements. Philosophers, he agreed with Moore, have certainly for some reason "'... been able to hold sincerely, as part of their philosophical creed, propositions inconsistent with what they themselves *knew* to be true'."[7] But if Moore is right in maintaining this, as he certainly appears to be, then the real problem, Lazerowitz argued, is "to see what it is about the *nature* of the views and the arguments used in their support that makes

---

[6] "Negative Terms," *Analysis*, Vol. 12, No. 3 (1952); reprinted in his book *The Structure of Metaphysics* (London: Routledge and Kegan Paul, 1955), p. 181. What I have said above regarding Ayer applies to Lazerowitz as well. Although his statement of Moore's position and criticism of it is superb, his subsequent analysis will strike many as extreme.

[7] *The Structure of Metaphysics*, pp. 3–4.

it possible" for them to do so. (p. 4) For obviously if such facts are well known to them, Moore's "refutations" (which consist in reminding them of this) are obviously not *refutations* – whatever else they may be.

That philosophers know what the facts are is perfectly plain (not that this is in doubt) from their behavior. Like everyone else, they consult their watches, keep appointments, carry on conversations with other people, and so on. Furthermore, they never seem to be struck by the absurdity of saying "none of *us* can really know that any human being besides himself exists," or of starting a lecture with the statement, "In the course of this lecture I propose to demonstrate the unreality of time'," which, it would seem, if Moore were right, they most certainly ought to be. And they are not struck by all this for apparently "not for a moment is the existence of other people or of temporal phenomena in question. If they were in question the proponents of the views could not fail to *see* the absurdity." (p. 9) Regardless, therefore, of what such philosophers hold academically, such facts are obviously never really in question – philosophers apparently knowing them even while expressing their views. But how is this possible?

It is possible, Lazerowitz replied, because metaphysical views are the sorts of things which can be neither proved nor disproved, confirmed nor disconfirmed. And they admit of no such confirmation or refutation because they are neither *empirical* (that is, they do not purport to tell us something that can be confirmed or disconfirmed by sense-experience, and therefore empirical facts cannot be brought to bear against them, such facts being simply irrelevant) nor *a priori* (that is, they do not purport to tell us what such words as "Time," etc. mean, and therefore counter-arguments or statements to the effect that by "Time" we do after all mean this or that, is also irrelevant to them). But if metaphysical views can be classified as neither empirical nor *a priori*, what then are they?

They are, Lazerowitz answered, "verbal recommendations." They are proposals with regard to the use of ordinary expressions. When a philosopher asserts something about, say, "Time" or "Reality," he is not, Lazerowitz explained, trying to communicate some information to us either about things or about words (he is not, that is to say, making either an empirical observation or an *a priori* one); he is recommending a change regarding our use of words about things. And it is because this is so that no counter-arguments based on an appeal to things or actual usage is relevant and can count against them. This is what Moore unfortunately failed to see.

But, of course, it does not obviously look as if this is what philosophers have really been doing. But the reason for this, replied Lazerowitz, is plain:

Instead of saying "Let us not use the word 'time' (or the word 'now'), let us
delete it from the language," he says "Time is unreal," and so creates the impression that he is framing theories *a priori* or empirical ... This creates the
illusion that they are "theories," and gives rise to the attendant puzzling stale-
mates. He does the same with his "proofs" and so furthers the illusion that he is
concerned to establish the truth of theories. (p. 20)

But this is all a mistake. For all the metaphysician is really trying to do
is to introduce certain innovations of a linguistic sort.

But why should the metaphysician wish to do that? Certain concealed psychological motives, Mr. Lazerowitz replied, compel him to it.
Philosophers, he explained, have a certain sub-conscious *uneasiness*
about some words and they try to rid themselves of this uneasiness by
either reforming these words or doing entirely away with them.

The fact is that:

For some people the word "change" in addition to its ordinary meaning, which
they do not give up in their everyday conversation, has the private meaning of
"catastrophic change." They make the unconscious equation change = dreaded
change; and they reassure themselves with the assertion, which is backed by the
verbal necromacy of a metaphysical proof, that their *status quo* will not be disturbed by a new situation which, whether justifiably or not, is felt to be menacing.
The hidden sense of the philosophical statement, Nothing really changes, is No
changes which would create anxiety in me are real. (p. 70)

And the same is true of those philosophers who have maintained (like
Heraclitus, for example) that, on the contrary, change alone is real.
Their behavior too can easily be accounted for, and on the same
principles. Like their antagonists, they too are burdened with unconscious needs and fears. In them, however, the fear of change is
simply replaced by its opposite – a tendency to change continuously.
And this is reflected in their obsession with it. "It is safe to say that
philosophers who, on the surface, say that change alone is real have
made the unconscious equation change = disarmed, harmless change,
which they substitute for the equation, change = dire change; and by
'proving' to themselves, and to others as well, that change is real they
produce the conviction that it holds no real menace." (Pp. 71–2)

It is, finally, however, the equation of "change" with "death" which
is involved in these linguistic innovations.

"The utterance 'Everything changes,' which means to us that all
things perish and pass away, may for one thing express a psychological-

ly concealed recognition of the unalterable fate meted out to us is impartially meted out to everyone: 'Everything changes' = 'Everyone dies.' Our sense of aloneness and outraged injustice is lessened by the feeling that our lot is the common lot, and it also gives us aggressive satisfaction" (p. 77) – a satisfaction grimly expressed, for example, on a headstone in Hartfield, Massachusetts, which reads:

> Death is a debt
> To nature due
> I have paid mine
> And so must you.

This is obviously a rather different kind of explanation as to what leads certain philosophers to speak nonsense from the sort provided, for example, by Ayer. Nonsense is regarded by it, as we have just seen, not necessarily as a function or product of language *per se,* but rather as a manifestation of a person's pressing psychological needs. Certainly these needs express and reveal themselves in language (for how else should it do so where philosophers whose business is words are concerned?) but, it argues, this is misleading, for such manifestations are simply symptoms whose disease is to be found elsewhere. That being so, the cure, of course, cannot consist in treating its symptoms. On the contrary, success here can be achieved only at a deeper level. That, at least, is what Lazerowitz seems to be saying.

In any case, these are, briefly and inadequately, some of the strange things which have been said in the last thirty or so years about philosophy and how it "comes to be written." It should perhaps be added that Ayer and Lazerowitz are not the only or perhaps not even the best representatives of this particular moment in recent philosophical history. Still they are representative of it – the former of the purely linguistic strain in it, the latter of its purely clinical strain. It should perhaps also be pointed out that this moment has had a richer and more varied career than I have here attempted to convey. Certainly that is the case with the *Blue Book* where these two divergent themes vie for our attention. It is to that work that I should now like to turn to see how these two themes or strains fare there.

3

But to summarize first: As we saw, recent linguistic or analytical philosophy begins with the death of British Idealism. Its death, we saw, was
the result of a curious question, namely, What has led philosophers to
say some of the very strange things for which they are so noted? Now
although Moore was the first to raise this question, he himself did not
answer it. Drawing their inspiration from other sources, especially from
Wittgenstein, some analysts argued that the trouble lay in language
which somehow had confused and misled these philosophers or metaphysicians. Ayer's remarks about Heidegger is a case in point and
representative of the sorts of things said by those of the *linguistic* wing
of the analytic school. To other analysts, however, this seemed too
superficial a diagnosis. Drawing heavily, like the others, from Wittgenstein, they argued that what doomed philosophers to speak nonsense
was something deeply psychological. This manifests itself in language
and can be approached in this manner, but it was not something
strictly or simply linguistic. An extreme representative of this *clinical*
wing of the analytic movement is Lazerowitz.

These strange things which analysts have said, now too require
explanation. Furthermore, although both wings stem from Wittgenstein and are both connected with his basic thesis regarding the way we
have been led into confusion "by means of language," there is reason to
believe that he has been misrepresented and his doctrine misunderstood.
An examination of its source or sources (as the case may be) may throw
light on this. Such an examination is especially important now, for this
doctrine of Wittgenstein's regarding the way we have been led into
confusion by language seems to be losing ground rapidly[8] and another
opportunity to see precisely what it contained or what it was meant to
contain may not soon occur again.

Our immediate problem, therefore, is to see what precisely this theory
regarding language is which gave rise to this strange flowering in the
hands of both types of analysts. Since its immediate source is Wittgenstein's *Blue Book*, our immediate task is to examine that work. The
theory, however, has other antecedents and in the subsequent chapters
an attempt will be made to see what these are and what light they cast
upon this page in recent philosophical history.

[8] See, for example, Warnock (p. 115), whose response and reservations regarding this
doctrine are typical of more recent attitudes.

CHAPTER TWO

THE DILEMMA OF THE *BLUE BOOK*

I

Ever since its publication in 1958, readers of the *Blue Book*[1] have been struck by the peculiar and incomparable qualities of that little book. Some have even come to regard it as Wittgenstein's best single work.

The *Blue Book*, Professor Ayer says of it:

Has a liveliness and freshness, even a clarity, which the *Investigations* lacks. In my opinion, this is one of those instances in which the preliminary sketches are aesthetically more successful than the resulting pictures: the picture has suffered from the painter's unwillingness or inability to stop retouching it. As compared with the English version of Wittgenstein's other published works, these *Blue and Brown Books* gain something also from the fact that they are not translations. Apart from a very few corrections which the editors have made, the English is Wittgenstein's own. It has the energy and fluency of the English which he spoke.[2]

The *Blue and Brown Books*, a review in the London *Times Literary Supplement*, states:

Are not just aids to the study of a superior book. Indeed there are probably many who will deny that they are inferior to *Philosophical Investigations*. Certainly they are written more imaginatively than the later work, and they have a freshness and directness that it does not have. This is, of course, partly because they did not have to undergo a long process of elaboration. But there is also another reason for it: they belong to the period when Wittgenstein had recently found a different way of approaching philosophical problems, and they are obviously written with a feeling of liberation, the feeling of someone who knows that he sees things in a new way.[3]

And Professor Newton Garver, reviewing the book in the journal *Philosophy and Phenomenological Research*, writes of it that:

---

[1] *The Blue and Brown Books, Preliminary Studies for the Philosophical Investigations,* (London: Basil Blackwell).

[2] *The Spectator* 201 (Nov. 14, 1958), p. 654.

[3] (Jan. 16, 1959), p. 36. The review is not signed.

The *Blue Book* strikes me as the best portal to Wittgenstein's thought. Occasional passages (e.g. 36–37) illuminate the *Tractatus*, and it stands to the *Investigations* as *De Intellectus Emendatione* does to Spinoza's *Ethica*: the style is more conventional, the general aim is clearer, and much refinement and detail is missing ... The overall impression is both charming and challenging.[4]

And, finally, Professor G. J. Warnock, who in his own book *English Philosophy Since 1900* had criticized Wittgenstein for too narrowly diagnosing the sources of philosophical problems,[5] says the following of the *Blue Book* in his review of it in *Mind*:

There is also some welcome variety in his remarks on the sources of philosophical puzzlement. Whereas later he seems to have wished always to say that we are led into perplexities by, or by means of, language, here he envisages from time to time several evidently different ways in which we may be mis-led. Philosophers sometimes attempt to copy the procedures of scientists: often they are betrayed by pressing analogies too far: they are apt to operate too boldly with inflexible categories: they are liable to be hypnotized by mechanical models; and in general they are prone to hastiness, over-tidiness, over-simplification. If so, a philosophical study of the workings of language will be valuable, not necessarily as leading to the source of philosophical problems in general, but at least as furnishing by example a uniquely powerful corrective to inveterate tendencies to misrepresent and to mis-assimilate.[6]

For a book of dictated notes, this is indeed high praise. But this little book is not only all that these writers have said of it; it is also, I believe, a good deal more. For although the unique qualities of this unusual and unique book as the clearest, best, and most revealing introduction to Wittgenstein's later thought has not gone unnoticed, what has so far failed to catch our eye are its unique qualities as our clearest, best, and most revealing introduction to the inner tensions and conflicts in the foundations of that thought. In what follows I should like to trace some of these tensions and conflicts, tensions and conflicts which as we noted in the last chapter, left their mark on the thought of the time to which it gave rise.

2

"One may say," Wittgenstein remarks regarding the *Blue Book*, "that what in these investigations we were concerned with was the grammar of those words which describe what are called "mental activities":

---

[4] Vol. 21 (1960–61), p. 576.
[5] See p. 115.
[6] Vol. 69 (1960), p. 284.

seeing, hearing, feeling, etc." (p. 70) "I have been trying in all this to remove the temptation to think that there '*must* be' what is called a mental process of thinking, hoping, wishing, believing, etc., independent of the process of expressing a thought, a hope, a wish." (p. 41) What prevents us from seeing what thinking, hoping, wishing, believing, etc., really are, is certain "established forms of expression" which mislead us into believing in these various mythical faculties and occult phenomena. But if language is somehow responsible for these various beliefs of ours – and the difficulties they bring with them – then it is also to language that we must turn in order to extricate ourselves from them. Going through such a process of analysis "rids us of the temptation to look for a peculiar act of thinking, independent of the act of expressing our thoughts and stowed away in some medium. We are no longer prevented by the established forms of expression from recognizing that the experience of thinking *may* be just the experience of saying, or may consist of this experience, plus others which accompany it." (p. 43)

What are these "forms of expression" which mislead us in this way, and how do they come to do so? These are some of the questions to which Wittgenstein directs himself in this little book.

The book, however, is very difficult to follow, and this for several reasons. It is written, first of all, in a kind of "stream-of-consciousness" style, with ideas arising, falling away and re-appearing, as in a reverie. Sometimes, ironically, an argument is suddenly dropped because in the course of it a word equivocally suggests a new – albeit not *entirely* unrelated – topic. A good example of this appears on p. 45 where the figurative statement (following upon a brief discussion of "personal experience"), "We seem to have made a discovery – which I could describe by saying that the *ground* on which we stood and which appeared to be firm and reliable was found to be boggy and unsafe," leads him in the very next paragraph to discuss the question whether objects (tables, for example) are solid or not, and what the scientist means when he declares them to be composed of tiny particles. "We have been told by popular scientists that the *floor* on which we stand is not solid, as it appears to common sense, as it has been discovered that the wood consists of particles filling space so thinly that it can almost be called empty."[7] This is not an isolated example.

---

[7] My italics. One of the reasons for such seemingly odd occurrences is, of course, the fact that the *Blue Book* was not really intended for publication, but consisted of notes which Wittgenstein dictated to his students. (See the Editor's Preface to the *Blue and Brown Books*,

This quality of the writing makes the work extremely difficult to grasp. The reader often finds himself puzzled as to why he is suddenly confronted with *this* particular issue, and why the matter just dealt with has suddenly been dropped – probably just as the point where he was beginning to get some notion of it. Furthermore, some issues which do not seem to weigh very heavily in the total scheme of the work seem to be discussed in great detail; others, seemingly more important than these, more briefly. This imbalance in the material adds enormously to one's difficulties. The result is that it is extremely difficult to know *how* to read the book.

Nor are these difficulties the reader's alone. Part of it lies with Wittgenstein himself, for he himself seems undecided as to the ultimate orientation of the work. Sometimes he seems to proceed as if he believed his chief concern is the proper analysis of some problem or other (e.g., solipsism, personal identity, sensation, etc.) At other times he seems to proceed as if, on the contrary, his main theme is the nature of philosophy or language and that these particular problems have been brought in merely as illustrations, and are therefore to be regarded as incidental to his main purpose, and so on.

Yet for all that the work does not lack a certain unity. It begins by dealing with the problem of the nature of the "process" called "thinking." Since the mistake we generally make about this process is repeated with other "processes" as well (e.g., "believing," "expecting," "sensing," etc.) a discussion of these other matters finds its place here too. But what is characteristic of our mismanagement of these concepts is characteristic, the argument is, of the whole enterprise of philosophy, and so the question arises, What has gone wrong in philosophy? The book is an attempt to answer this question.

3

Turning to the *Blue Book*, we find Wittgenstein asking himself, almost at the opening, this curious question: "If I give someone the order 'fetch me a red flower from that meadow,' how is he to know what sort of flower to bring, as I have only given him a *word*?" Would it help us to say that the word causes him to have a certain image (say, an image

---

p. v). On the other hand, it would be a mistake, I think, to regard the *Blue Book* as simply or merely notes. They were certainly more than that, as is indicated by the fact that he had stencilled copies of them made and even sent a copy to Russell.

of a red flower) which serves him as a guide and pattern? The answer is no, for I could of course have given him the order "*imagine* a red flower," and we would, by parity of reasoning, be forced to suppose that before carrying out *this* order he must have imagined a red flower to serve him as a pattern or guide for the red flower which he was ordered to imagine, which is absurd. Well, then, what is it to understand words?

We are inclined to say that it cannot be merely a matter of using words, that this cannot be all there is to "thinking." Are there not, we say, "*certain definite* mental processes" involved in the use of language, processes which give life to the signs of language and without which language could not function? And is the function of these signs not, after all, to arouse in us those processes and activities which give them life – activities which take place in the mind, that "queer medium" that is able to bring about effects (how, we do not quite understand) but one certainly not possible, as we are inclined to say, to a *material* mechanism alone?

These two ideas (that the mind is a kind of queer, occult mechanism, and that in themselves words or signs are lifeless) are obviously bound up together. For it is our belief that no amount of adding of dead or inorganic signs to other inorganic signs can give them life that leads us to say that what must be added is something immaterial, something arising from quite a different medium. But let us see now, however, whether this addition of the immaterial can bring the dead signs to life, or whether, ultimately, we are not really compelled to say that the life of the sign resides simply in the *use* we make of it in the system of language.

Let us, then, consider somewhat more closely this imagist theory of language. If, as that theory claims, thinking is a matter of having images which give life and meaning to our words, then let us imagine a case where, instead of our responding to the word "red," say, by conjuring up a red image, we were somehow equipped to produce the red thing itself or some picture or sample of it. (Wittgenstein imagines the absurd case of a man carrying around with him in his pocket a chart with colored squares). Here – as absurd as this illustration may perhaps be – there certainly would be no loss of vividness (if that is the determining factor here), for, on the contrary, the visual image we would now get would be more vivid than the one we might imagine or produce from our memories. Now the question is, "if the meaning of the sign (roughly, that which is of importance about the sign) is an image built up in our minds when we see or hear the sign, then – why should the written sign

plus this painted image be alive if the written sign alone was dead?"
(p. 5) And the answer is, of course, that it isn't any more alive now than
it was before. But if that is so, doesn't the occult quality which we
supposed to be attached to the imagined sign somehow vanish from
sight and is no longer able to impart life to anything at all? Isn't this
occult quality, in other words, simply a fiction now? Certainly it no
longer seems able to perform the job for which it was designed. Obviously, then, to try to save "thought" by positing a stream of images will
not do. These images being again simply signs will require still other
signs to give them life, and so on.

Why, then, are we so tempted to believe that language involves such
further, occult processes – processes without which, as we are inclined
to say, the signs of language are dead and lifeless? Wittgenstein's
answer to this question is that we are tempted to believe this because of
the mystifying effect on us of our language. We tend to think of the use
of the signs of our language, he says, as if they were objects *co-existing*
with the signs, and, correspondingly, of such mythical processes as
"thinking" as similarly co-existing with such processes as talking, etc.
"A substantive," he says simply, "makes us look for a thing that
corresponds to it." (p. 1)

But this is all a mistake. For "thinking is essentially the activity of
operating with signs." "This activity is performed by the hand, when
we think by writing, by the mouth and larynx, when we think by
speaking; and if we think by imagining signs or pictures, I can," he
says, "give you no agent that thinks." (p. 6) However, if you should say
"that in such cases the mind thinks, I would," he adds, "only draw
your attention to the fact that you are using a metaphor, that here the
mind is an agent in a different sense from that in which the hand can
be said to be the agent in writing." (Pp. 6–7)

What makes it difficult for us to see this is that the existence of the
word "mind" leads us to look for a thing corresponding to it, and then
to assign to it (because it is so intractable) all sorts of occult powers.
This is an error which "recurs again and again in philosophy," (p. 6)
and is "one of the great sources of philosophical bewilderment." (p. 1)
On the one hand we feel, in such cases, that we can't point to anything
as the referent of these metaphors (which is understandable since there
is nothing really to point *to*) yet we also feel we ought to be able to do
so. It is out of such dilemmas and the "mental cramp" they produce
that metaphysical theories (which are really pseudo-theories since the

problems for which they are designed as "solutions" are pseudo-problems) generally arise.

Thus, in the case we are now considering, having once assigned a referent to the metaphor "mind" (regarded as a kind of agent of thought) we become puzzled as to why we can get to know so little about it, and this leads us to construct all sorts of theories as to why these things are so difficult to understand. In the case of the mind, this leads us to regard it as a very peculiar and strange medium, especially so since in its case (as we further go on to say) we are dealing apparently with something that is able to bring about astonishing effects. It is in this way that we now begin, misguidedly, to search for answers to questions which were not really the ones that began to puzzle us. For after all, as Wittgenstein points out, we were not puzzled, or we did not begin to ask, How does the mind perform this or that activity? but, What is talking, thinking, etc? "What struck *us* as being queer about thought and thinking was not at all that it has curious effects, which we were not yet able to explain (causally)." (Pp. 5–6) Our problem was a philosophical one and not a scientific or psychological one. But the existence of the word or metaphor together with the various associations that it has for us traps us into dealing with it as if it were a scientific question.

And this is typical of philosophical investigations, at least as they have been carried on in the past. Led to believe that we are dealing here with scientific-like problems, we try to solve them in the way a scientist might hope to do so. When we don't succeed (as is only to be expected, for our problems, not being scientific ones, do not lend themselves to this type of handling) we become puzzled. This in turn gives rise to all sorts of theories which only lead us further astray and increase our bewilderment.

It is the same, for example, with the ancient problem regarding Time. Trying to solve this problem in the way we might try to solve the problem regarding, say, the "ultimate constituents of matter," and not succeeding very well only reinforces our original prejudice that these philosophical entities are queer sorts of things and "that here are things hidden, something we can see from the outside but which we can't look into." (p. 6) "And yet nothing of the sort is the case. It is not new facts about time which we want to know. All the facts that concern us lie before us. But it is the use of the substantive "time" which mystifies us," (p. 6) and misleads us into dealing with it in an impossible way. If we will look into the "grammar" of that word we shall no longer be puzzled and will know quite well how to use it. And that is all we mean by it.

But, unfortunately, the question, What is Time? which so puzzled Saint Augustine, like ordinary scientific questions, appears to ask, says Wittgenstein, for something else – for a definition, perhaps, or information. But how, Wittgenstein enquiries, would a definition help us here? A definition would only lead us to other undefined terms. And besides "why should one be puzzled just by the lack of a definition of Time, and not by the lack of a definition of "chair?" Why shouldn't we be puzzled in all cases where we haven't got a definition?" (p. 26)

It is obviously then not the want of a definition which is the cause of our puzzlement here, but something else. We do not see this because the puzzlement expresses itself here in a misleading way by means of a question-form "What is ... ?" But this is simply, if we recognize it properly, an utterance of "unclarity, of mental discomfort ... comparable with the question "Why?" as children so often ask it" – a question which like "What is ... ?" "doesn't necessarily ask for either a cause or a reason" (p. 26) but is simply an expression of puzzlement.

It is little wonder, therefore, that such questions or puzzlement cannot be relieved or answered by providing information but only by coming to recognize its cause, with lies in certain "contradictions" in the grammar of the words used. "Augustine, we might say, thinks of the process of measuring a *length*: say, the distance between two marks on a travelling band which passes us, and of which we can only see a tiny bit (the present) in front of us." (p. 26) Thinking of time in terms of such an analogy – of such a picture embedded in the notion of "measuring" common to the two cases – he naturally became puzzled as to how it could be done; how, that is, it should be possible for one to be able to measure it. For the past, as he put it, can't be measured, as it is gone by; and the future can't be measured because it has not yet come; and, finally, the present can't be measured, for it has no extension. What, then, *is* Time?

To solve this puzzle, obviously what we must do is come to see that we mean quite a different thing by "measurement" when applied to a distance on a moving band, with the grammar of the word when applied to Time. It is because we try to apply the word rigidly and consistently and find that we cannot, that we run up against difficulties and become bewildered. We fail to see that we are really a victim here of a kind of equivocation, that the same word may have quite different meanings when used in different contexts. "The problem may seem simple, but its extreme difficulty is due to the fascination which the analogy between two similar structures in our language can exert on us." (p. 26) Like children, we find it hard to believe that one word can have two meanings. (p. 26)

Wittgenstein goes on to generalize this point. "Philosophy, as we use the word, is a fight," he says, "against the fascination which forms of expression exert upon us." (p. 27) It is an attempt "to counteract the misleading effect of certain analogies." (p. 28) "The man who is philosophically puzzled sees a law in the way a word is used, and, trying to apply this law consistently, comes up against cases where it leads to paradoxical results." (p. 27) Sometimes we think a definition is what is wanted, and we give one only to discover that it doesn't work. And so we think we gave the wrong one; that some other one will work better. The fact of the case, however, is that there simply is no such thing as a single correct definition. Perhaps suspecting this we come to think that we simply don't know what these words ("mind," "time," "knowledge," etc) mean, and that therefore, perhaps, we have no right to use them.

But words simply "have those meanings which we have given them; and we give them meanings by explanations." (p. 27) Nor is it true that all words have strict meanings. They do not, and this is neither a defect in them, nor a sign of a "deplorable lack of clarity" in us. And it isn't that, for "in general we don't use language according to strict rules." It has not, he says, been taught to us in that way either. "Philosophers very often talk about investigating, analysing, the meaning of words. But let's not forget that a word hasn't got a meaning given to it, as it were, by a power independent of us, so that there could be a kind of scientific investigation into what the word *really* means. A word has the meaning someone has given to it." (Pp. 27–8)

"There are words," he continues, "with several clearly defined meanings. It is easy to tabulate these meanings. And there are words of which one might say: They are used in a thousand different ways which gradually merge into one another." (p. 28) In our discussions, however, we "constantly compare language with a calculus proceeding according to exact rules," (p. 25) – despite the fact that our ordinary use of language "conforms to this standard of exactness only in rare cases." (p. 25) What we must do therefore is to undermine and loosen this rigidity of mind and counteract the effect which these misleading analogies have upon us.

To accomplish this, it is not enough simply to "enumerate actual usages of words." We must also "invent new ones, some of them because of their absurd appearance."[8]

---

[8] The case of the man with the colored chart in his pocket would, I suppose, be an example of such an invention.

It is in this connexion that he now mentions, for the first time, the notion of "language games." "These are ways of using signs," he explains, "simpler than those in which we use the signs of our highly complicated everyday language." In these simpler structures we gain the advantage of seeing our "forms of thinking ... without the confusing background of highly complicated processes of thought." In these simpler forms "the mental mist which seems to enshroud our ordinary use of language disappears. We see activities, reactions, which are clear-cut and transparent." Since these simple processes are not separated by a break from our more complicated ones, we shall be able to "build up the complicated forms from the primitive ones by gradually adding new forms," (p. 17) and in this way locate the source and nature of the difficulties which are responsible for our puzzlement.

But "when we say that by our method we try to counteract the misleading effect of certain analogies, it is important," Wittgenstein warns us:

That you should understand that the idea of an analogy being misleading is nothing sharply defined. No sharp boundary can be drawn round the cases in which we should say that a man was mislead by an analogy. The use of expression constructed on analogical patterns stresses analogies between cases often far apart. And by doing this these expressions may be extremely useful. It is, in most cases, impossible to show an exact point where an analogy begins to mislead us. Every particular notation stresses some particular point of view. (p. 28)

"The cases," however, "in which particularly we wish to say that someone is misled by a form of expression are those in which we would say: 'he wouldn't talk as he does if he were aware of this difference in the grammar of such-and-such words, or if he were aware of this other possibility of expression' and so on." (p. 28)

For example:

We talk of kinds of number, kinds of propositions, kinds of proofs: and, also, of kinds of apples, kinds of paper, etc. In one sense what defines the kind are properties, like sweetness, hardness, etc. In the other the different kinds are different grammatical structures. A treatise on pomology may be called incomplete if there exist kinds of apples which it doesn't mention. Here we have a standard of completeness in nature. (p. 19)

But when we turn to mathematics and try to achieve a similar completeness and definiteness, the result proves disastrous, as is shown by those mathematicians who misguidedly have tried to make certain exclusions and divisions in their discipline.

Thus we may say of some philosophizing mathematicians that they are obviously not aware of the difference between the many different usages of the word "proof"; and that they are not clear about the difference between the uses of the word "kind," when they talk of kinds of number, kinds of proofs, as though the word "kind" here meant the same thing as in the context "kinds of apples." Or, we may say, they are not aware of the different *meanings* of the word "discovery," when in one case we talk of the discovery of the construction of the pentagon and in the other case of the discovery of the South Pole. (pp. 28–9)[9]

The "kinds" of thing dealt with here are quite different and therefore the analogy between them can carry us only a short distance. One can, of course, draw a sharp boundary here if one wishes, and by means of it make all the divisions and exclusions one desires, but this boundary "will never entirely coincide with the actual usage, as this usage has no sharp boundary." (p. 19) And what actual usage tells us here is that there are many "kinds" of thing which lack such sharp boundaries, and are not distinguished by the possession of some one feature common to all its members.

On the contrary, the belief that in order to get clear about the meaning of a general term one has "to find the common element in all its applications" has "shackled philosophical investigations." Not only has it led to no result but it has:

Also made the philosopher dismiss as irrelevant the concrete cases, which alone could have helped him to understand the usage of the general term. When Socrates asked the question, "What is knowledge?" he does not even regard it as a *preliminary* answer to enumerate cases of knowledge. If I wished to find out what sort of thing arithmetic is, I should be very content indeed to have investigated the case of a finite cardinal arithmetic. For (a) this would lead me to all the more complicated cases, (b) a finite cardinal arithmetic is not incomplete, it has no gaps which are then filled in by the rest of arithmetic. (Pp. 19–20)

To show that concepts have no very sharp borders but rather share a family likeness, he goes on here to examine what it is "to expect someone from 4 to 4:30." It cannot, he points out, be simply assimilated to some one particular thing. There are, he says, "endless variations to this process which we all describe by the same expression." (P. 20) Furthermore, the experience, being an enormously varied one, may be described not only in different but sometimes even in strange and unusual ways. Nor is there anything wrong with that, as long as we give our expressions meaning and make it clear how we are using them. But, unfortunately, here too such innovations sometimes mislead us into believing all sorts of absurd things.

---

[9] See also in this connexion his remarks – on pp. 23, 57–8 and 64 – concerning some of the other confusions generated by these words.

For example:

It might be found practical to call a certain state of decay in a tooth, not ac-
companied by what we commonly call toothache, "unconscious toothache" and
to use in such a case the expression that we have toothache, but don't know it.
It is just in this sense that psychoanalysis talks of unconscious thoughts, acts of
volition, etc. Now is it wrong in this sense to say that I have toothache but don't
know it? There is nothing wrong about it, as it is just a new terminology and can
at any time be translated into ordinary language. On the other hand, it obviously
makes use of the word "to know" in a new way. (Pp. 22–3)

But unfortunately the new expression not only leads us to think that
we have done more than we actually have but it also calls up "pictures
and analogies which make it extremely difficult for us to go through
with our convention." (P. 23) And this in turn creates puzzlement and
gives rise to bad philosophy.

Thus by the expression "unsconcious toothache," for example, we
are:

Misled into thinking that a stupendous discovery has been made, a discovery
which in a sense altogether bewilders our understanding; or else you may be
extremely puzzled by the expression (the puzzlement of philosophy) and perhaps
ask such a question as "How is unconscious toothache possible?" You may then
be tempted to deny the possibility of unconscious toothache; but the scientist
will tell you that it is a proved fact that there is such a thing, and will say it
like a man who is destroying a common prejudice. He will say: "Surely it's quite
simple; there are other things which you don't know of and there can also be
toothache which you don't know of. It is just a new discovery." You won't
be satisfied, but you won't know what to answer. (P. 23)[10]

But obviously what has been overlooked by these two disputants is,
inter alia, the fact that these other things we "don't know of" are things
which, unlike having a toothache, we "don't have." And what puzzles
us is the fact that since a toothache is something "we have," we ought,
normally speaking, "know of it." The new notation, although not un-
intelligible, does not seem to provide room for this, and thus runs into
conflict with the old. This generates confusion and puzzlement.

It is the same with the new "sense data" terminology which "has
deluded people into thinking that they had discovered new entities,
new elements of the structure of the world, as though to say 'I believe
that there are sense data,' were similar to saying 'I believe that matter
consists of electrons'," (p. 70) whereas all they have really done is to
invent a new terminology, a new way of speaking. Nor is it any different with the so-called "discoveries" of psychoanalysis and all the
disputes and confusion which this has caused. "'Can we have unconsci-

10 See also here his discussion on pp. 45–6.

ous thoughts, unconscious feelings, etc?" The idea that we can has revolted many people. "Others again have said that these were wrong in supposing that there could only be conscious thoughts, and that psychoanalysis had discovered unconscious ones." Both, however, were confused about what had really happened. "The objectors to unconscious thought," for example,

Did not see that they were not objecting to the newly discovered psychological reactions, but to the way in which they were described. The psychoanalysts on the other hand were misled by their own way of expression into thinking that they had done more than discover new psychological reactions; that they had, in a sense, discovered conscious thoughts which were unconscious. The first could have stated their objection by saying "We don't wish to use the phrase 'unconscious thoughts'; we wish to reserve the word 'thought' for what you call 'conscious thoughts.'"; They state their case wrongly when they say: "There can only be conscious thoughts and no unconscious ones." For if they don't wish to talk of "unconscious thought" they should not use the phrase "conscious thought," either. (Pp. 57–8)

These disputes and difficulties can be cleared up by recognizing that they are essentially verbal, that what is being disputed are not the facts of the case – whatever they may be – but simply their description.

That a good deal of philosophizing is, however, of this sort is illustrated by the long-standing controversy over the problem of Solipsism. As in the other cases that we have investigated the trouble here is that neither the Idealist nor the Realist is really aware as to what they are asserting or objecting. The Solipsist, on the one hand, is unaware that he is really only asserting a "grammatical" proposition and not an "experiential" one; and the Realist, on the other hand, is unaware that he is really only objecting to the former and not to the latter, and that his objection is therefore really irrelevant. On the contrary, his reply, which he states by saying "that surely there is no difficulty in the idea of supposing, thinking, imagining that someone else has what I have," (p. 48) just brings out the difficulty." For the one who argues like this, Wittgenstein points out, "overlooks the difference between different usages of the words 'to have' and 'to imagine'." (p. 49)

"A has a gold tooth" means that the tooth is in A's mouth. This may account for the fact that I am not able to see it. Now the case of his toothache, of which I say that I am not able to feel it because it is in his mouth, is not analogous to the case of the gold tooth. It is the apparent analogy, and again the lack of analogy, between these cases which causes our trouble. And it is this troublesome feature in our grammar which the realist does not notice. (P. 49)

The point, however, is this. "It is conceivable that I feel pain in a tooth in another man's mouth; and the man who says that he cannot feel the other's toothache is not denying *this*." (p. 49) For when he asserts that he 'can't feel another's pain he is not asserting an experiential proposition. He is, without realizing it, simply making a *grammatical* statement. What he is really saying is something like this: the reason why it is not possible to experience another's pain is not because it is physically impossible to do so, but simply because it is *his* pain and therefore absurd to suppose that it could be *yours*. "I may have toothache he might have put it, "in another man's tooth, but not *his* toothache." (p. 53) *That* only *he* can have.

The objections of the Realist are thus completely beside the point. He does not notice that A's toothache which the Solipsist denies that we can feel, is not *in* A in the same way in which we might say the gold tooth, that we cannot see, is. Nor is the Solipsist himself, Wittgenstein adds, really aware of it either. It may be impossible for us, in other words, to see the gold tooth because it is hidden in his mouth. If it were not thus hidden we could easily see it. But no analogous reason lies behind our impossibility of feeling his toothache. *That* we can never feel, regardless of what experiments we might try. What both of them seem to fail to see, in other words, is that the two impossibilities "differ in their grammar where at first sight they might not seem to differ." (P. 53) Having the same experiential form, each of them is led to believe that what is being stated is "a kind of scientific truth" (P. 55) when as a matter of fact what is being stated or debated in the philosophical proposition (i.e., in the statement "I can't feel his toothache") is only something "grammatical."

The same difficulty may be illustrated, for example, in the case of the word "same." "We use the phrase 'two books have the same colour,' but we could perfectly well say: 'They can't have the *same* colour,' because, after all, this book has its own colour, and the other book has its own colour too." (P. 55) Similarly with the statement "The colours green and blue can't be in the same place simultaneously." Here too we might come to feel that what we are asserting is that there is a kind of physical barrier lying between the two colours, that somehow they are in each other's way and that this is why they cannot both be in the same place simultaneously. But that is not at all the case, for we are not here dealing with physical impossibilities; what we are really stating is only a "grammatical rule" and a logical impossibility.

This confusion of the grammatical with the experiential is what leads philosophers to say typically metaphysical (i.e., paradoxical) things. It is also what leads them to believe that they have somehow stumbled upon some very striking scientific or empirical discoveries when as a matter of fact they have merely used words in consistently and therefore systematically misleading ways. If there is anything actually new that they have accomplished here it is to forge some new conventions regarding the uses of words, and speaking about them. In the case of the word "same," for example, it is obviously not in accordance with ordinary usage to say that "this book can't have the *same* color as that one," because we do use the word "same" in that way (i.e., in that vague and loose sense which permits us to say this.) The philosopher, on the other hand, would like, apparently, to restrict the use of the word in such a way (making it mean not "similar" but "the *very* same") so that it would be absurd to suppose that "this book could have the *same* colour as that book" – for obviously on this more restricted usage *this* book "can't" have the same color as *that* book, for that book has the color which it has, and this one has the color which *it* has! But to do this, or to say this, is only to create new linguistic conventions; it is not to say or discover anything new or startling about any of the things described by them. In the end it is simply a matter of making new notations. Philosophers, however, have not as a rule been aware that is all that it is.

4

I have presented Wittgenstein's account without comment in an attempt to capture something of the flavor of the original which depends so much upon the cumulative effect which his numerous examples and illustrations tend to have on us and the way in which he allows different strands of argument to combine and support each other. These different strands and the examples and illustrations which support them, although striking, are not without their difficulties.

Perhaps an unfair kind of criticism to make of his argument that philosophy has often gone astray because it has regarded all words as if they were substantives (or names) would be that the "philosophy" in question is none other than his own. Although to say this may seem at first ungenerous there is, of course, a great deal of truth to this remark. For where else could one find such a highly developed name theory of language, which he is here in the *Blue Book* so busy exposing, than in his own early work, the *Tractatus*? On the other hand to say this is not entirely fair either, for Wittgenstein was not, of course, the sole architect of that curious theory of language. It was, after all, the peculiar brain child of Logical Atomism and was to be found not only in the works of the early Russell but also in Frege, in Moore and in Meinong, where (according, at least, to Ryle's well-known account) it did in fact lead (as Wittgenstein argues here on general principles that it must) to the belief in the objective existence of all sorts of abstract and fictional *entia rationis*. Ryle's argument here, together with his account of the history in modern times of this strange doctrine of language, has been so well traced by him in his justly acclaimed paper "The Theory of Meaning" that I will not take the reader's time to review it here. Such considerations, however, do not entirely answer all the objections one is here inclined to raise.

For, first of all, Wittgenstein made that doctrine his own and must not therefore be so easily excused from responsibility for it. His folly here, in other words, need not be at all revealing either about language or philosophy as such but may be peculiar to him alone. Secondly, even if it is true (although this is doubtful) that the only philosophers Wittgenstein knew intimately were Russell, Moore, Frege and Meinong, these obviously are not the whole of philosophy, so that even if what Ryle says does apply to them, it may not apply to others. And so Wittgenstein is again not justified in blaming philosophy or philosophers for this peculiar folly. Thirdly, even if it would be possible to widen Ryle's list, this would still not prove that there is any kind of intimate causal connexion between holding a name theory of language and being led to believe in the objective existence of *entia rationis*. No one in the history of philosophy, for example, is better known for holding a name theory of language than Hobbes, yet no one was more suspicious of the objective existence of abstract entities than he. On the contrary, analysts have even tended to regard him as rather anticipating their own theories.

But, finally, we might ask (what has so often been asked in this connexion) whether Wittgenstein has not really inverted the process he describes? No doubt we now are helped to frame such concepts as "mind," "time," etc. by the existence of these substantives in our language, but that was not, after all, the case with those who were first to invent these words. What led them to devise these words was no doubt certain motives and experiences which they wished to fix and perpetuate and obviously not the words in question which did not yet exist. Now they may have been mistaken about these experiences and misled by them (and since they continue to be operative with us, we may be misled by them too) but that is certainly different from being misled by "words" as such. Wittgenstein's doctrine that one of the causes of philosophical bewilderment is the existence of "substantives" (which "makes us look for a thing what corresponds to it") is therefore, I think we must say, far from convincing.

But although Wittgenstein may be wrong in thinking that this kind of error "recurs again and again in philosophy," he seems to have something much more interesting to say regarding the second kind of confusion which he takes up in the *Blue Book* – I mean the confusion between the philosophical and the empirical, of which, according to him, philosophers have also frequently been guilty. Again, it is difficult to say what philosopher or philosophers Wittgenstein has in mind here. He seems to think, apparently, that once having made the first mistake the second inevitably follows. Looking, for example, as he explains it, at the "mind" as if it were the *name* of some independently existing entity, leads naturally to the attempt to deal with it in the sorts of ways that have proven successful in dealing with other such empirical problems. Since no such simple referent can be found here, this leads us to try to rationalize our failure by inventing all sorts of pseudo-psychological theories regarding the mind's mysterious operations, its intractability, etc. This relieves our puzzlement but the theories in question, according to Wittgenstein, are neither philosophical nor empirical but simply nonsensical. That is, as we saw, Wittgenstein's account of this second kind of confusion which he believes takes place here.

Now although there are a number of questions which one would very much like to ask Wittgenstein regarding the precise mechanism which leads to this further kind of confusion, the case is, I think, different with the distinction he is led to make here between the purely philosophical question and the purely empirical or scientific one. On this matter, Wittgenstein has, I believe, some very illuminating things to say. They have to do, I think, with the general distinction we now make between science and philosophy. Although it has been common practice for some time now to distinguish between these two, for many people it is still far from clear how and where, precisely, the lines should here be drawn. And here Wittgenstein is indeed very helpful. It has to do with what he says about the distinction between the philosophical "What is ...?" and the empirical "What is ...?"

Now, according to Wittgenstein, a question is simply a linguistic phenomenon. Some questions refer, of course, to things beyond them and can be settled extra-linguistically, that is, empirically. There are, however, other kinds of question, ones which look very much like the first and which we are tempted to answer in the same way but which somehow do not lend themselves to such solutions. One of the reasons they do not admit of such a solution is because, unlike them, they do not point to anything beyond them – to anything extra-linguistic – but have their source solely in language. For example, there exists in our language the word "meaning" and this is a word which we ordinarily and intelligently apply or predicate of such other words as "propositions" or "sentences" – saying, for example, that that sentence has "meaning," etc. At other times, however, we are tempted to apply this word ("meaning") to words such as "life" – asking ourselves, for example, such questions as "Does life have meaning?" Here we are confronted with a question which we do not quite know how to answer or what to make of it, and this puzzles us. What Wittgenstein, I believe, would say here is that to apply the word "meaning" to "life" is to misapply it and to come up with an impossible question. It may now be difficult for us to see that this *is* an illegitimate question, for having used this word in this context so often, it no longer appears strange to us. But it is the sort of question which we do not come by independently and objectively but is one rather that is suggested by and is a by-product of language itself. Our language, being what it is, makes it possible and makes it seem intelligible to ask this question too, but it is certainly not one answerable in the ways in which similarly constructed questions can be answered.

But this does not necessarily mean that all such questions are non-sensical. Being a by-product of the way in which the world of our experience is arranged and organized in our language and language being the mirror through which we view the world, there can be nothing trifling about any of the questions suggested by it. In other words, these are *real* questions. They do not, however, apply to any kind of noumenal reality. On the other hand, since language is a human construction, and words have the meanings we give them, we must also remember that there is nothing ultimate about the view of the world suggested by it, nor of the questions it tends to raise. Furthermore, since language did not develop in any rational way but is a free growth, it should not surprise us that it should daily confront us with so many dilemmas. Philosophers who try to bring into it more consistency than it can accommodate simply make matters worse. The consistency which they try to bring to language merely creates further paradoxes and involves them in squabbles with other people (whether these are scientists, other philosophers, or simply ordinary people), squabbles which on close inspection turn out to be simply verbal. What they seem to lack is that initial insight that philosophical questions, unlike empirical questions, are not about an external reality but rather either about the conceptual schemata (or language) we use in organizing that external reality or are by-products of the friction brought about by conflicting schemata – that they are, in either case, only about language. Unlike empirical problems, therefore, these problems can only be settled by showing how a particular word is being misused, how it comes to be so misused, what its true use is, etc., etc.

Now insofar as Wittgenstein stresses the difference here between the scientific and the philosophical and tries to show how certain problems admit of only a linguistic solution and should not be confused with scientific problems which are quite different from them, he was giving expression to some very important insights, insights not out of keeping with the whole trend of recent philosophy which, certainly ever since Kant (if not Locke) has been moving in this direction. Of course Wittgenstein thought philosophers themselves had been confused over this. Had he known the history of philosophy better he would have been surprised how sympathetic that history was towards his point of view – at least on this matter. For modern history of philosophy is a history of the successive attempts to define the categories and modes of operation of the mind, and Wittgenstein's own attempts clearly form part of this overall effort.

In saying all this we must not, of course, lose sight of the differences. His orientation is, for example, entirely different from theirs. First of all, his investigation, rather than tending to elevate philosophy, tends on the contrary to elevate science; secondly, unlike them again, what he seems above all to be interested in is to show, not how the philosophical question forces us to deal with the issues at a deeper level and enables us to provide answers which are rationally satisfying to the mind, but rather how these two questions – the empirical and the philosophical – have been confused. This emphasis gives an entirely different tone to his work. But this is where, also, I think, one finds his account so puzzling. And one finds it so for two separate reasons: one very general, the other rather more specific. Let us consider these in turn.

Wittgenstein, as we have seen, would like us to believe that certain questions ("What is the meaning of life?," for example) are initially made possible by language itself – that is, we form them on analogy with such other questions as "What is the meaning of this sentence?," etc. Since this latter question can be answered straightforwardly, we assume that the other question can also be answered in this way. But "meaning" is not a word we can meaningfully apply to such a term as "life" and that is why, unlike the question "What is the meaning of this sentence?," we find it so difficult to answer. It is of course enormously difficult for us now to believe that such a question as "What is the meaning of life?" has no straightforward answer but is simply a pseudo-question, suggested to us initially by other structurally similar questions in our language. But that is so because, he would say, we have become so accustomed to using the word meaning in this context too that it no longer strikes us as queer or absurd, which, however, strictly speaking, it is. To see its queerness now requires a kind of radical re-adjustment, a kind of total change in us, for this would require seeing that the whole question is senseless and should never have arisen in the first place, and at the present stage in our linguistic history all our instincts are against our seeing this. Were we able to make this total readjustment, were we able to return to this former state, we would then be able to regard that combination of words just as absurd as we now do the combination "round square." The question, that is to say, would simply make no sense.

Now suppose we were somehow able to make this adjustment and see the question in the way Wittgenstein would predict we would see it, would that mean that we would no longer be bothered by what is implied by it? The answer here is of course that if we were truly able to turn our minds around in this drastic way, then the thought that is implied by that question would probably then never occur to us. That being so, one begins to wonder what else such a change would imply. Could one, first of all, change one's linguistic habits in this drastic way? And if one could, could one do so without undergoing other profound changes as well? For this is not a matter of pretending that the question "What is the meaning of life?" is absurd, but rather of seeing, sincerely and with complete conviction that it makes no sense and that one has not the least idea what it could possibly mean. It seems highly doubtful that one could make this kind of total readjustment and still remain what one is. For, of course, that is not the only use of "meaning" nor the only question we would be compelled to give up. We would have to give up a good many other things too. Before long we would discover that our language had greatly diminished in size, and with it also our lives and minds.

Has this question then – the question "What is the meaning of life?"– the same ultimate and referential sense which ordinary empirical questions have? Even if we granted Wittgenstein that it has not and agreed with him that it is language itself which initially makes this question possible (even suggests it to us) we would still not need to agree that the question is nonsensical. Language makes many other things possible as well, and although these other things too many lack that kind of reality which only empirical sentences possess they are not for that reason either negligible nor unreal.

But to turn now to some of the more particular objections his account tends to raise in our minds.

Wittgenstein wants us to believe that philosophical problems about time (how it is that we can measure it, for example) arise because we tend to apply to the concept inappropriate criteria, such criteria as, for example, a band travelling between two marks. Augustine, he believes, was so misled. But what empirical evidence, we might ask him, is there for this? But perhaps it is not the sort of thing which he would wish to see settled empirically. But if so, then what is it about the language of time which makes confusion here inevitable? Does this inevitableness, for example, come simply from the fact that, like children, we find it hard to believe that one word can have two meanings? Certainly in the case of philosophers whose daily bread is words this is too unbelievable to be believed. Wittgenstein would not, I think, wish to rest his case on that. Upon what, then shall we rest it?

From the account so far given of Wittgenstein's thought I do not believe one can answer this question. Whether Wittgenstein had, in fact, an acceptable answer to it is hard to say. What we can say is that although it is certainly possible for anyone (including Augustine) to be confused about anything at all as a result of thinking about it along mistaken lines (in terms of inappropriate analogies, for example) this is far different from claiming that thinking about it along such lines is *inevitable*. This applies, I think, to all of Wittgenstein's examples: to the physicists who have been tripped up by the word "solid"; to the mathematicians who have been deceived by the words "proof" and "kind"; the psychoanalysts who have played fast and loose with the words "unconscious" and "discovery"; and the philosophers who have been misled by such words as "sense data," "knowledge," etc.

There are numerous other questions of this sort which the account of Wittgenstein's *Blue Book* that I have so far given raises. But all of them are overshadowed, it seems to me, by a certain major internal difficulty or contradiction in the work itself. This difficulty involves certain other themes and ideas that are to be found in this book and which seem to conflict with those we have already described. These are not, to be sure, sustained in the way in which the dominant theme summarized in the last section is, but they make themselves felt all the same and very powerfully at that. It is to this that I now wish to turn.

5

Now it is Wittgenstein's thesis in those parts of the *Blue Book* summarized above, as we have seen, that the confusion which abounds in philosophic discourse is due directly to language. That is where, apparently, according to him, our difficulties begin and where, consequently, their resolution must also take place. Nor does he leave us in doubt about this. "We must not be misled," he tells us early in the book, "by the similarity of their linguistic form into a false conception of their grammar" (p. 16) "When words in our ordinary language have prima facie analogous grammars we are inclined to try to interpret them analogously; i.e. we try to make the analogy hold throughout"; (p. 7) "a metaphor ... misleads us." (p. 41) There are a great many other such statements, some of which I have already had occasion to quote.

There is, however, really no need to appeal to other statements of this sort, for Wittgenstein himself, early in the book, has provided us with what appears to be a kind of summary of his argument and which reveals, although somewhat obscurely, what he regarded the main line and structure of it to be. Our difficulties, he expresses it there, (p. 17) are due to "our craving for generality." This craving, he says there, "is the resultant of a number of tendencies[11] connected with particular philosophical confusions"; (1) "the tendency to look for something in common to all the entities which we commonly subsume under a general term," (p. 17) forgetting that such entities are not united by one property common to all but are rather like a family with overlapping likenesses; and (2) "our preoccupation with the method of science" and

---

[11] Although Wittgenstein goes on to list four such tendencies, the second and third are really expansions of the first, and so there are in effect really only two.

the temptation "to ask and answer questions in the way science does."
(p. 18) Uniting again these two strands into one, he states finally:
"Instead of 'craving for generality' I could also have said 'the contemptuous attitude towards the particular case'," each of which has,
as we unfortunately fail to realize, its own individual linguistic character.

Now some of this is, of course, not very clear. This is especially so
with regard to the notion "craving for generality." But the rest of what
he says and especially about the matter of our attitude to the particular
case is highly revealing. For not only does it explain why the *Blue Book*
should contain the great number of analyses of individual words and
expressions ("particular cases") which it does[12] but it also makes it
clear why the argument should be structured in the way it is – going, as
we have seen, from the confusion of words to the confusion of the
grammatical with the scientific, which in turn generates puzzlement,
etc. But this now poses a problem of some dimensions. For aside from
the fact that these examples (to say nothing of those which other
analysts have since added) seem extremely vulnerable to close inspection, their place in the line and structure of his argument seems to
conflict, as I have already mentioned, with another strand in it which
seems of almost equal importance.

Although the existence of such a different theory regarding the nature
and origin of philosophical puzzlement makes itself felt most definitely
towards the conclusion of his discussion of Solipsism, echoes of it may
be heard earlier and elsewhere.

"We destroy the outward similarity," he says, for example, on p. 55,
"between a metaphysical proposition and an experiential one, and we
try to find the form of expression which fulfils a certain craving of the
metaphysician which our ordinary language does not fulfil and which,
as long as it isn't fulfilled, produces the metaphysical puzzlement" –
implying thereby, I believe, that there are sources of puzzlement (this
"certain craving") which are not simply a product of linguistic confusion. "We are in all such cases thinking of a use," he says further:

Different from that which our ordinary language makes of the words. Of a use,
on the other hand, which just then for some reason strongly recommends itself
to us. When something seems queer about the grammar of our words, it is because
we are alternately tempted to use a word in several different ways. And it is
particularly difficult to discover that an assertion which the metaphysician makes

---

[12] Needless to say, I have not managed to include in my outline of the *Blue Book* all of them.
The *Blue Book*, of course, contains a good deal else that I have not mentioned.

expresses discontentment with our grammar when the words of his assertion can also be used to state a fact of experience. (p. 56)

Here, apparently, we are given to understand that confusion arises not only from our attempt to use different words in consistently similar ways, as had been suggested earlier, but rather, vice versa, from our tendency to use similar words in different ways. And furthermore, the difficulty, he suggests again, is not so much the metaphysician's as ours, for here apparently it is less a matter of the metaphysician falling victim to the deceptions of language as his curious discontentment with it (which is, of course, quite a different thing from his being misled by it).

In connexion with this last point, however, Wittgenstein goes on to reaffirm his former position by stating that the metaphysician is not aware that he is really only objecting to a linguistic convention. But on this rather important point too he seems undecided. "The trouble with the realist," we find him saying in one place, "is always that he does not solve the difficulties *which his adversaries see*, though they too don't succeed in solving them," (p. 48)[13] And at another: "This is one of the things which the *person feels dimly* who is not satisfied with the explanation that though you can't know ... you can conjecture ..." (p. 54) And finally, somewhat cautiously: "... the philosopher who says this *may well think* that he is expressing a kind of scientific truth ..." (p. 55) Apparently although not entirely alive to what he is about, the metaphysician (as these passages seem to suggest) is not entirely in the dark about it either. In view of his dominant theme (namely, that the metaphysician is a person blindly victimized and led astray by language) these remarks must strike us as extremely perplexing.

But although intimations of the existence of such a different theory regarding philosophical confusion are to be found elsewhere in the book, its most explicit statement appears in connexion with his discussion of Solipsism. We have already had occasion to examine some portions of this discussion, but it is what he adds further to them that is interesting and puzzling. Let us therefore turn to them.

"When the solipsist says," Wittgenstein remarks here, "that only his own experiences are real, it is no use answering him: "Why do you tell us this if you don't believe that we really hear it?" Nor must we believe that by answering him in this way, we have really solved his difficulty. And there is no use believing this, he says, for there is simply no common sense answer to a philosophical question:

[13] Italics here and in the next two quotations are mine.

One can defend common sense against the attacks of philosophers only by solving their puzzles, i.e., by curing them of the temptation to attack common sense; not by restating the views of common sense. A philosopher is not a man out of his senses, a man who doesn't see what everybody sees; nor on the other hand is his disagreement with common sense that of the scientist disagreeing with the coarse views of the man in the street. That is, his disagreement is not founded on a more subtle knowledge of fact. We therefore have to look round for the *source* of his puzzlement. (Pp. 58–9)

And we find "that there is puzzlement and mental discomfort," he says, "not only when our curiosity about certain facts is not satisfied or when we can't find a law of nature fitting in with all our experience, but also when a notation dissatisfies us – perhaps because of various associations which it calls up." (p. 59)

Our ordinary language, which of all possible notations is the one which pervades all our life, holds our mind rigidly in one position, as it were, and in this position sometimes it feels cramped, having a desire for other positions as well. Thus we sometimes wish for a notation which stresses a difference more strongly, makes it more obvious, than ordinary language does, or one which in a particular case uses more closely similar forms of expression than our ordinary language. Our mental cramp is loosened when we are shown the notations which fulfil these needs. These needs can be of the greatest variety. (p. 59)

Just what these needs are which drive the metaphysician or Solipsist to revise language in this drastic way is not very clear from the passages which follow. What is interesting about all this, however, is not the particular reasons (whatever they are) which "irresistibly tempt" the metaphysician to try to revise language in this way, but rather the fact that his temptation is not now any longer ascribed to such things as misleading metaphors and analogies but rather to such things as "mental cramp," confinement, rigidity of language, and so on. It is not now, that is to say, the philosopher's rigidity and his blindness to the deceptions of language which makes him say strange and paradoxical things; language itself is now seen to have something rigid and confining in it – inducing the philosopher to try to change it.

But although this is so, Wittgenstein not only discusses these new "confusions" (if we may still call them that) in the same light as the earlier ones but seems to prescribe the same cure for them as well. Metaphysicians who fall victim to this sort of malady, he says, "are in all such cases thinking of a use different from that which our ordinary language makes of the words," (p. 56) and the thing to do therefore is to show them how the words in question are actually used in our language. For here too the metaphysician is guilty of confusing the grammatical with the empirical. For obviously, he goes on to argue here:

The man who says "only my pain is real," doesn't mean to say that he has found out by the common criteria – the criteria, i.e., which give our words their common meanings – that the others who said they had pains were cheating. But what he rebels against is the use of *this* expression in connexion with *these* criteria. That is, he objects to using this word in the particular way in which it is commonly used. (p. 57)

"On the other hand," says Wittgenstein, "he is not aware that he is objecting to a convention." (p. 57) He simply "sees a way of dividing the country," he says, "different from the one used on the ordinary map."

He feels tempted, say, to use the name "Devonshire" not for the county with its conventional boundary, but for a region differently bounded. He could express this by saying: "Isn't it absurd to make *this* a county, to draw the boundaries *here*?" But what he says is: "The *real* Devonshire is this." We could answer "What you want is only a new notation, and by a new notation no facts of geography are changed." It is true, however, that we may be irresistibly attracted or repelled by a notation. (We easily forget how much a notation, a form of expression, may mean to us, and that changing it isn't always as easy as it often is in mathematics or in the sciences. A change of clothes or of names may mean very little and it may mean a great deal.) (Pp. 56–7)

Now as interesting as all this no doubt is, it seems to me that what he says here is only loosely connected with the sources of confusion and puzzlement which form the dominant theme of this book. It may well be, of course, that in the end there is confusion in both cases, but it is, however, quite a different thing to say that a man is led into confusion by the peculiar structure of language, from saying – as he now appears to be doing – that certain deep urges and dissatisfactions with existing expressions leads him to revise them in such a way that confusion results. *That* argument seems to have an entirely different structure. Is this confusion then, we might ask, a product of the metaphysician's inattentiveness to language, or is it (as the second argument seems to suggest) a product of his supersensitivity to it? These are obviously two quite different things.

Nor is this all. For if, as the second argument asserts, the metaphysician is led to revise language because of its constricting effect upon him, then it is really no use to show him how the words in question are actually used in the language, for obviously that is precisely what he is objecting to. And if that is so then, of course, it cannot be the case that he is, as Wittgenstein asserts, unaware of it. After all that is why he wishes to revise it! Of course what Wittgenstein states is that he is unaware that this is *all* he is really doing. But then Wittgenstein himself cannot mean that either, for if that is all a revision of language amounts to, then the "craving" is indeed of a very peculiar sort. But obviously Wittgenstein himself must believe that by rearranging the map we do more than merely rearrange lines and shadows. No doubt we do not change any of the geography in this way, but we do certainly change our view of that geography. And that is obviously what the metaphysician desires – as Wittgenstein seems to be well aware. But that is also, however, quite a different thing from being led into confusion by the peculiar deceptions and structure of language.

In a sense what this finally comes down to is the question whether the various tendencies connected with particular philosophical confusions, of which Wittgenstein speaks in his summary, are the *results* of "our craving for generality" (meaning that certain other pressures within us lead us to these perplexing results), as this second theory seems to imply, or whether "our craving for generality" (whatever that may mean) is, on the contrary, the resultant of them; whether, that is to say, these confusions are to be regarded as *symptoms* of this general tendency in our nature or are to be regarded as the causes of it. In view of what is at stake here this is not an uninteresting technical question.

Now it can be said, I think, that it is Wittgenstein's general view in the *Blue Book* (despite the parallel argument which seems to conflict with it) that this "craving for generality" of which he speaks early in the book is, as he states it there, the resultant of these various confusions and tendencies. Yet when one takes into consideration what he has said about the difficulties in detecting just where an expression begins to mislead and also what he says in the *Brown Book* and the *Philosophical Investigations* about philosophical confusions being a product of a "one-sided diet,"[14] of our tendency to take our "ideas" and "language" from only one kind of example,[15] – to say nothing of the fact that the number of purely linguistic examples illustrative of philosophical confusions drastically diminishes in the subsequent works where the argument is made less and less dependent on them[16] – then

[14] *Philosophical Investigations* I, 593. Translated by G. E. M. Anscombe. (Oxford: Basil Blackwell, 1953).

[15] *Brown Book*, p. 150.

[16] They also tend to be less colorful and seem to be introduced not so much with a view to showing how they have tended to confuse and mislead, but rather in order to illustrate his main doctrine regarding Essentialism. It is also interesting, perhaps, to note that in the *Brown Book* – with the exception of one passage on p. 109 – the grammatical/experiential confusion does not seem to play an important role either. This point, of course, is revealing in still a different way as well. For the gradual disappearance of the grammatical/experiential distinction, about which so much is made in this work, may have been due to the fact that he came to see that the dangers of construing language as a "calculus" (in the way Russell, Logical Positivism, and he himself in the *Tractatus* has been in the habit of doing) were even greater than those resulting from confusing metaphysical propositions with scientific ones.

I think it becomes clear that he was beginning to suspect that perhaps philosophical confusion has a deeper source, one not simply *linguistic* – although often issuing in that.[17]

6

What this source is and why he tends to speak of it in the way he does and with that sense of doom which he seems to think attaches to it, are questions not easy to answer on the basis of a merely internal examination of his works. Yet these seem important questions, ones, unfortunately, which as it seems to me, Wittgenstein himself never succeeded in resolving. His students, he apparently thought, succeeded even less so. On the contrary, they seem to have aggravated the problem, finally inducing him to publish his own thoughts, despite his own dissatisfaction with them.

"Up to a short time ago," he writes in the Preface to his *Philosophical Investigations* in, I believe, this connexion:

I had really given up the idea of publishing my work in my lifetime. It used, indeed, to be revived from time to time: mainly because I was obliged to learn that my results (which I had communicated in lectures, typescripts and discussions), variously misunderstood, more or less mangled or watered down, were in circulation. This stung my vanity and I had difficulty in quieting it.

And further: "For more than one reason what I publish here will have points of contact with what other people are writing today, – If my remarks do not bear a stamp which marks them as mine, – I do not wish to lay any further claim to them as my property."

These are very severe remarks and they force us to ask what it was in their work that he found so objectionable. What this is is not easy to say. But as with so much else in Wittgenstein it probably has to do with what he conceived the nature of philosophy and its proper task to be.

As we have see, he thought its task was, as he expresses it in the *Philosophical Investigations*, to unmask absurd theories. Philosophers had arrived at nonsense by trying to say what cannot be said and by running their heads "up against the limits of language." They had

---

[17] I do not mean to imply by this that the *clinical* wing of recent analytic philosophy (as that is represented, for example, by Lazerowitz) is therefore truer or closer to Wittgenstein's thought than the strictly *linguistic* wing or approach might be said to be. All I am interested in pointing out there is that such a further source of philosophical puzzlement is given in the *Blue Book* and that it tends to conflict with the more dominant theory of the book.

built for themselves "houses of cards" upon the "ground of language" and it was now time to demolish them by clearing up this ground upon which they stand. Philosophy is thus a "battle against the bewitchment of our intelligence by means of language"; a battle to be won by "assembling reminders" and by bringing "words back from their metaphysical to their everyday use."

But how, now, according to Wittgenstein, we might ask, does this "bewitchment of our intelligence by means of language" take place? Is it a matter,[18] say, of running afoul of the use of the word "nothing" upon which, according to Ayer, Heidegger's metaphysics (or perhaps only those portions of it which he quotes) is sustained? Is Moore's refutation of Mill's "proof" of Utilitarianism an example of it? Is the supposition that "history" has a goal towards which it "marches" (a supposition which, according to one recent writer, is a product of the fallacy of Figure of Speech)[19] illustrative of it? Is it that sort of thing? It would be tempting to say that this is not what Wittgenstein means. But there are textual sources in Wittgenstein not only for most of these suggestions,[20] but, as we have now seen, for countless others like them.

But although this is quite true, it is also true, I think, that this is not *all* that Wittgenstein means. His work contains various strains and is rich and complex. With the possible exception of his attack upon Essentialism (which is a theme common to all his works) they tend, on the whole, to be non-committal, cautious, exploratory. They are also, however, as we have seen, extremely puzzling, the argument pointing in divergent and sometimes misleading directions.

But although in comparison with it the work of others may seem like a "mangling" and "watering down," I think we can see that his work lends itself very easily to this. Nor was he necessarily unaware of this.[21] This was, I believe, one of the sources of his own deep dissatisfaction with it, as well as the reason for the various different attempts to produce a book which would be free of these dangers and would convey

[18] To give only some *linguistically* oriented examples.

[19] See *What is Philosophy? A Short Introduction* by Elmer Sprague (New York: Oxford University Press, 1961), p. 128.

[20] See, for example, the *Brown Book*, pp. 107–8.

[21] See, for example, *Tractatus* (London: Routledge & Kegan Paul, 1961), 4.1121: "Does not my study of sign language correspond to the study of thought-processes, which philosophers used to consider so essential to the philosophy of logic? Only in most cases they got entangled in unessential psychological investigations, and with my method too there is an analogous risk." What I have in mind here, however, is not so much the psychological or psychoanalytic emphasis put on Wittgenstein's work, as the purely linguistic one. Wittgenstein, however, was aware of this danger as well, as I shall have occasion to note later.

in a faithful way the spirit of his thought. Neither the *Blue Book*, nor the *Brown Book*, nor finally the *Philosophical Investigations*, obviously manages to do this. These are not simply drafts of the sort one makes in the process of writing a book. Each of them is a fresh attempt to put the products of his discoveries in their true light.

What these are it is possible to see better, I think, against the wider background of some literary parallels and sources to which I now wish to turn. For just as his work tends to illuminate for us the writings and work of those who took their inspiration from him, so similarly the work of his own literary and philosophic predecessors (Spinoza, Kant, Schopenhauer) from whom he took *his* inspiration tend to illuminate his own writings.

7

But first I should like to review briefly what it is I have tried to say in this chapter.

As stated in the last chapter, one of the major sources of the doctrine which is the subject of this study is Wittgenstein's *Blue Book*. This is a difficult and puzzling work. Some of these difficulties are no doubt due to its seeming formlessness and its constantly shifting centre of gravity. Still the work does not lack a certain unity. Beginning by dealing with the nature of "thinking," it goes on to show that what is characteristic of our mismanagement of this concept (a mismanagement which leads philosophers to say the very odd things for which they are so noted) is characteristic of our mismanagement of other concepts as well, and in fact of the whole enterprise of philosophy. What is this characteristic, and how has it been responsible for these curious confusions? The book is an attempt to come to grips with this question.

As we have been led to believe, and as an abstract of Wittgenstein's argument indeed shows, the confusions, according to him, which abound in philosophic discourse have their origin in language. The philosopher, according to his argument here, is a man who, misled by language, propounds with perplexing results essentially linguistic propositions as if they were empirical or scientific ones. What leads him to make this confusion and, as a result, to say the very strange things he does, are certain misleading words and expressions and the structurally iso-morphic analogies embedded in them. In order to dispel this confusion and relieve the puzzlement, what we must do is to destroy "the out-

ward similarity" between the two propositions that are wrongly assimilated. This can be done by seeing "how the words in question *are actually used in our language*" and thus how and where they mislead.

What this means and how much of it can meaningfully be assimilated
by one looking at it historically can only be suggested in a preliminary
way at this point. Certainly Wittgenstein's attack on the name theory
of language seems to lack force; on the other hand, his discussion of the
distinction which this leads him to make between the philosophical and
empirical seems to represent an important advance over previous
efforts to grapple with this problem and tends to bring greater clarity
to it.

But although this dominant theme and strand of the *Blue Book* does
certainly lend itself to this kind of extension and interpretation, there
is to be found in it, strangely enough, another strand which seems to be
in direct conflict with it. What this new strand seems to assert is that
philosophical puzzlement, far from being the *effect* of linguistic confusion is, on the contrary, itself the very cause of it! Certain deep dissatisfactions with language, the argument now is, leads the philosopher
to revise it in ways more congenial to him. What these dissatisfactions
are precisely which leads the philosopher to reform language (in what
prove to be misleading ways) is not made very clear here. What does
seem to be clear, is that language alone is now no longer to be regarded
as the sole villain. Something else, something obviously deeper and
more intractable is apparently responsible.

What this is and why Wittgenstein tends to speak of it in the way he
does and with that sense of doom which he apparently thinks attaches
to it, are questions not easy to answer on the basis of a merely internal
examination of his works. This strand of his argument is the source of
that *clinical* wing of recent analytic philosophy (just as the dominant
strand is the source of the purely *linguistic* wing of that movement) and
the division between them (as well as their relations) simply reflects the
division which exists in this work itself; but for a better understanding
of the significance of this contradiction in the work, as well as its own
differences with those which it fathered, we must turn elsewhere.

CHAPTER THREE

KANT

Although Wittgenstein's debt to Kant has not failed to catch the eye of some of his readers, its true depth and extent has still to be recorded. Nor is the existing literature on this point very illuminating. On the contrary, considering the already vast scope of this literature, the references to Kant are not only often lacking in interest but are in the majority of cases simply not there at all. In what follows I should like to describe in more detail than has yet been attempted the nature and extent of this relation and what, as I see it, is particularly interesting and illuminating about it.

I

Before proceeding to do this, however, it might be well to review and summarize what we already know regarding this relation. Dividing the existing materials on this matter into three separate classes – A) Works on Wittgenstein's early period; B) Works on his later period; and C) Works on his philosophy as a whole – the materials concerned are as follows:

A 1. Anscombe, G. E. M., *An Introduction to Wittgenstein's Tractatus,* London: Hutchinson, 1959.
  2. Stenius, Erik, *Wittgenstein's Tractatus: A Critical Exposition of Its Main Lines of Thought,* Oxford: Blackwell, 1960.

* This was written before the appearance of Professor Stephen Toulmin's remarkable essay "Ludwig Wittgenstein" (*Encounter,* (January, 1969), pp. 58–71) in which he anticipates a good many of the conclusions reached in this and the other chapters of this book. Another recent paper which the reader should consult in this connection is Professor J. Hartnack's valuable study "Kant and Wittgenstein" (*Kant Studien,* (Heft 2, 1969), pp. 131–4). Professor Hartnack's paper, too, came to my attention after the completion of my study.

3. Maslow, Alexander, *A Study in Wittgenstein's "Tractatus,"* Berkeley and Los Angeles: University of California Press, 1961.

4. Black, Max, *A Companion to Wittgenstein's Tractatus*, Ithaca: Cornell University Press, 1964.

5. Favrholdt, David, *An Interpretation and Critique of Wittgenstein's Tractatus*, Copenhagen: Munksgaard, 1964.

6. Griffin, James, *Wittgenstein's Logical Atomism*, Oxford: Clarendon Press, 1964.

7. Copi, Irving M., and Beard, Robert W., (eds.), *Essays on Wittgenstein's Tractatus*, New York: The Macmillan Co., 1966.

B 8. Pole, D., *The Later Philosophy of Ludwig Wittgenstein*, London: University of London, The Athlone Press, 1958.

9. Pitcher, George (ed.), *Wittgenstein: The Philosophical Investigations*, Garden City, New York: Anchor Books, Doubleday & Co., 1966.

C 10. Malcolm, Norman, *Ludwig Wittgenstein: A Memoir*, Oxford and New York: Oxford University Press, 1958.

11. Pitcher, George, *The Philosophy of Wittgenstein*, Englewood Cliffs, N.J.: Prentice-Hall, 1964.

12. Hartnack, J., *Wittgenstein and Modern Philosophy*, tr. M. Cranston, Garden City, New York: Anchor Books, Doubleday & Co., 1965.

13. Fann, K. T., (ed.), *Ludwig Wittgenstein: The Man and His Philosophy*, New York: A Delta Book, Dell Publishing Co., 1967.

Taking the last of the three classes of materials first, we find that no references at all to Kant appear in Hartnack (12 above), and only one in Malcolm (10 above).

The reference in Malcolm is to be found in Professor von Wright's memorable sketch which precedes Malcolm's own account and which had previously appeared in the October, 1955 issue of *The Philosophical Review* (Vol. 64, No. 4). Professor von Wright reports here that "from Spinoza, Hume and Kant he (Wittgenstein) said that he could get only occasional glimpses of understanding" (p. 21). Professor von Wright does not go on to say how or whether these glimpses affected Wittgenstein's own thoughts or writings. Believing, however, that "the author of the *Philosophical Investigations* has no ancestors in philosophy" (p. 15) and that this work is "without literary sources of influence" (*ibid.*) he must obviously be of the opinion that the influences, if any, did not go beyond the early work. In this he seems to be supported by Pitcher

(11 above) whose book (one half of which is devoted to the *Tractatus*, the other to the *Philosophical Investigations*) contains only one *direct* reference to Kant and this deals with a point made by Wittgenstein in the *Tractatus*. Pitcher brings to our attention here (p. 147) that Wittgenstein's point in *Tractatus* 5.633 and 5.6331 – that just as it is impossible to see the eye which sees, so it is with the experiencing subject or self – is one which "has been expressed much earlier in the history of philosophy by Hume and Kant," although "Wittgenstein doubtless got it from his reading of Schopenhauer." Whether Pitcher means to imply by this that Wittgenstein could not have gotten it from Kant directly or that he did not read Kant, is not clear. Pitcher's next two references to Kant (on pp. 190 and 325) are of a general and passing nature – the former pointing out that Wittgenstein's philosophical *puzzles* are like Zeno's *paradoxes* and Kant's *antimonies*; the latter reporting on a remark made by Wittgenstein to Karl Britton[1] concerning his (Wittgenstein's) philosophic reading. Britton writes:

During the walk Wittgenstein assured me (laughing) that no assistant lecturer in philosophy in the country had read fewer books on philosophy than he had. He said he had never read a single word of Aristotle, although he had lately read much of Plato and with much profit. As for Hume and Kant, it was all very well for me to read them because I was not yet as experienced in philosophical thinking as he was: but he could not sit down and read Hume – he knew far too much about the subject of Hume's writings to find this anything but a torture.

Pitcher's last mention of Kant (p. 326) is again of a very general nature. It is this: although Wittgenstein's early and later works are in many ways enormously different, they nevertheless share the common goal of attempting to "mark out the limits of sense, to indicate the boundary between what can intelligibly be said and what cannot be said." And in pursuing this task, Wittgenstein "was carrying on, in his own way, the work started in modern philosophy by Locke, Hume and Kant."

Obviously not a very great deal of information is to be gleaned from these three works: nothing at all, as we have seen, from the Hartnack book; only the fact that Wittgenstein had dipped into Kant from the Malcolm book; and the undeveloped and hurried attempt to locate Wittgenstein within the philosophic tradition in the Pitcher book, in which we learn that 1) Wittgenstein's *puzzles* have their structural counterparts in the history of philosophy; as had indeed 2) his overall

---

[1] Pitcher quotes from Karl Britton's paper "Portrait of a Philosopher" which first appeared in *The Listener* (June 10, 1955). Although the paper is reprinted in Fann (13 above) I find it convenient to take note of it here. It is the only reference to Kant in Britton's paper.

task which is one that was begun by Locke, Hume and Kant; however that 3) he had no patience with Hume (and Kant?), knowing the subject matter of their philosophizing only too well himself; 4) the eye example being, perhaps, an instance of this.

A bit more information comes to us from the Fann book (13 above). This is the most recent publication of all, although of its thirty papers that it reprints only one is new, the rest having appeared elsewhere in a variety of journals. Since the collection has only recently appeared I should like to describe it in some detail. It contains, first of all, the biographical sketch by Professor von Wright (which we have already noted); it also reprints Professor Gilbert Ryle's memoir of Wittgenstein, which serves as a Preface to Copi's and Beard's collection (which I shall discuss below); and it reprints Norman Malcolm's and Paul Feyerabend's excellent and well-known papers (which appear as well in Pitcher's collection, to be discussed below). None of these latter three papers contains any references to Kant. Of the remaining twenty-six papers, no less than ten refer at one point or another to Kant. This number is however misleading since in the majority of cases such references are of a general and passing nature and are not interesting from our point of view here. As a matter of fact only six papers may be said to make a contribution to our topic. Of these six I have already mentioned Britton's paper and so I will now go on to report on the remaining five.[2]

Mays (in a paper entitled "Recollections of Wittgenstein") tells us that "Wittgenstein seemed to have little reading in the history of philosophy, although he had read St. Augustine, Pascal and Kant" (p. 84). "He once likened himself to Kant in a puckish sort of way," he informs us, "and he used to emphasize that philosophy was an activity rather than a subject" (p. 82). Heller (in a paper entitled "Wittgenstein: Unphilosophical Notes") tells us that "in talking about the stature of a philosopher," he remarked "that the measure of a man's greatness would be in terms of what his work *cost* him," and goes on to point out that "this is Kantian ethics applied to the realm of thought: true moral goodness was for Kant a victory over natural inclination, the costlier the better" (p. 92). Alice Ambrose (in a paper entitled "Wittgenstein on Some Questions in Foundations of Mathematics") begins by saying

---

[2] Since the book contains no index, it might be well to list here the authors and page numbers of *all* the references to Kant. They are: (von Wright) 27; (Britton) 60, 61; (Drury) 69; (Mays) 82, 84; (Heller) 90, 92, 96, 104, 106; (Bouwsma) 149; (Ambrose) 266; (Pitcher) 327; (Wisdom) 364; (Levi) 366, 368; (O'Brien) 390, 395.

that she will attempt to explain Wittgenstein by setting "a question which Wittgenstein did not formulate in precisely my fashion; but my formulation provides a springboard for the exposition of his treatment of problems intimately connected with it" (p. 266). The question, she says, is "similar to Kant's question about pure mathematics: How is applied mathematics possible?" (*ibid.*) Pitcher (in a paper entitled "Wittgenstein, Nonsense, and Lewis Carroll") points out (on p. 327) the resemblance between Wittgenstein's remarks (in the *Blue Book*, p. 13, for example), regarding acting *in accordance with* a rule and *obeying* or *following* a rule, and Kant's similar notions in the realm of ethics. And, finally, O'Brien (in a paper entitled "The Unity of Wittgenstein's Thought") points out in a footnote (on p. 395) that "the fact that 'logic' and 'a knowledge of objects' presents us with the scaffolding of the world suggests that even in the *Tractatus* 'logic' does not mean simply a formal study of inferences but is being conceived of more broadly, or more concretely, in the direction of the later sense of 'logic' in which certain *subject matters* determine a 'logic'. In Kantian language it is more like transcendental logic than formal logic."

Although the information provided by these sources is sketchy it is not unimportant. Later I shall have occasion to point out where it is that Kant says philosophy is an activity and not a subject and what else it was that Wittgenstein learned from Kant there. Mays's disclosure will prove to be valuable there in that it will provide external confirmation of what I hope to show by way of internal evidence alone. The attempt to draw parallels which is made by the other four writers indicate how far-ranging Kant's influence upon Wittgenstein may indeed have been, or how illuminating it may be to look at Wittgenstein through Kantian lenses. With perhaps the exception of Alice Ambrose's paper, however, the others are much too sketchy and undeveloped to succeed in either establishing this influence or providing the illumination sought.

Of the two titles listed in B above, Pole (8 above) makes no reference to Kant at all. Pitcher (9 above), a book which brings together some nineteen separate papers, contains two papers which do make such references: the first is a chapter by A. M. Quinton (excerpted from D. J. O'Connor, ed., *A Critical History of Western Philosophy*, London: Collier-Macmillan Ltd., 1964); the other a paper by Stanley Cavell (which first appeared in *The Philosophical Review*, Vol. 71 (1962) No.1). Quinton's first comment is that

broadly speaking, the *Tractatus* sets out a general theory of language in relation
to the world. It gives an answer to the Kantian-looking question: how is language,
and so thinking, possible? Wittgenstein was not, as Russell supposed in his
introduction to the book, projecting an ideal language in conformity with the
most stringent standards of logical perfection. He was attempting, rather, to
reveal the essential structure that must be possessed by any language capable of
being significantly used and which must, therefore, be hidden behind the familiar
surface of our actual language (p. 3).

Quinton's second and final reference (more a mention than a reference)
is of a passing and contrasting nature. I shall have more to say about
his first comment later on.

Cavell's remarks deal with a point we have already encountered in
Pitcher and, interestingly, here in Quinton. He adds a good deal to it,
however. Pointing out (p. 172) that Wittgenstein's view regarding "the
limitations of knowledge" (that they are not "barriers to a more perfect
apprehension, but conditions of knowledge *überhaupt*, of anything we
should call "knowledge")[3] bears an "obvious resemblance" to Kant,
he goes on a few pages later (pp. 175–76) to elaborate upon this. We
shall understand better, he remarks there, what Wittgenstein means
by "grammatical" knowledge if we keep in mind that it is the knowledge called by Kant "transcendental." That the two are similar he
shows by comparing the following two passages, the first from Kant,
the second from Wittgenstein.

And here I make a remark which the reader must bear well in mind, as it extends
its influence over all that follows. Not every kind of knowledge *a priori* should
be called transcendental, but that only by which we know that – and how – certain
representations (intuitions or concepts) can be employed or are possible purely
a priori. The term "transcendental," that is to say, signifies such knowledge as
concerns the *a priori* possibility of knowledge, or its *a priori* employment (*Critique
of Pure Reason*, trans. by N. Kemp Smith, p. 96).
Our investigation ... is directed not towards phenomena, but, as one might say,
towards the "possibilities" of phenomena (*Philosophical Investigations*, & 90).

Cavell goes on to bring some further evidence to bear upon this comparison.

As the "transcendental clue to the discovery of all pure concepts of the understanding" (*Critique*, pp. 105 ff.) Kant uses the idea that "there arise precisely
the same number of pure concepts of the understanding in general, as ... there
have been found to be logical functions in all possible judgments" (p. 113).

---

[3] Although Quinton is dealing with the *Tractatus* and Cavell with the *Philosophical
Investigations*, both are making a related point. Quinton is saying Wittgenstein was not attempting to define what it would be to possess an ideal or perfect language, and Cavell is
saying (among other things) that Wittgenstein was not attempting this with regard to knowledge.

Wittgenstein follows the remark quoted above with the words: "We remind ourselves, that is to say, of the *kind of statement* that we make about phenomena.
... Our investigation is therefore a grammatical one" (90). And where Kant
speaks of "transcendental illusion" – the illusion that we know what transcends
the conditions of possible knowledge – Wittgenstein speaks of the illusions produced by our employing words in the absence of the (any) language game which
provides their comprehensible employment (cf. & 96). ("The results of philosophy
are the uncovering of one or another piece of plain nonsense and of bumps that
the understanding has got by running its head up against the limits of language")
(& 119).

Quinton's and Cavell's comments are a good deal more helpful than those
reported on thus far. Quinton's remark that the *Tractatus* as a whole
deals with a Kantian-looking question is a bolder suggestion than anything made so far in the materials examined. It is also one, however, as
we shall see when we turn to the materials under A, which has indeed
been explored to a degree previously. It will therefore be discussed in its
appropriate place. Cavell's comments deal with the *Philosophical Investigations* and like Quinton's seem to be an effort to relate that work
as a whole (and not just this or that passage in it) to Kant. It is, as far as
Wittgenstein's later works are concerned, the only effort to do so that I
am aware of.[4] Since a good portion of this chapter will be taken up with
the connections to be found between Kant's *Critique of Pure Reason* and
Wittgenstein's later philosophical writings, I will say no more about
this at this point, but will rather go on to report of the materials under
A.

There are no references to Kant in Griffin (6 above) and only one
(of no importance, however) in Anscombe (1 above).

Turning to Copi and Beard we find that although they reprint some
thirty papers, Kant's name is to be found in only three of them. One is
no interest at all, another (in Richard J. Bernstein's "Wittgenstein's
Three Languages") merely points out that "Wittgenstein's ladder
language has affinities with Plato's dialectic, the language of Kant's
Critique, and Carnap's meta-languages" (p. 236); and the last (in a
paper by Gustav Bergmann entitled "The Glory and Misery of Ludwig
Wittgenstein") accuses Wittgenstein of inheriting his psychologism and
a priori-ism from Kant (see p. 351).

Favrholdt has a number of references to Kant but in the main they

---

[4] I have not, indeed, examined all the literature on Wittgenstein. However, the papers
collected in Copi and Beard, in Pitcher and in Fann (to say nothing of the books listed above)
represent a good portion of that literature. In addition, Kant's name does not appear in any
of the titles of papers to be found in K. T. Fann's extensive bibliography ("A Wittgenstein
Bibliography: Writings by and about Him." *International Philosophical Quarterly*, 7 (1967),
311–339) which lists well over six hundred titles. Still, of course, some other references have
no doubt escaped me.

are points which have already been mentioned either by Stenius or Maslow, to which I will turn in a moment. It should perhaps be mentioned that although he too finds a "great similarity" (p. 168) between Wittgenstein's conception of the "I" and Kant's conception of Transcendental Unity of Apperception, he thinks that it is "questionable whether Wittgenstein is in any way inspired by Kant." "I believe it to be more probable," he remarks, "that his views concerning the metaphysical subject have been inspired by Schopenhauer" (p. 169). Although this is the second denial of this kind that we have come across, I hope to show later on that much nevertheless remains which Wittgenstein could have gotten only directly from Kant.

Max Black points out, first of all (doing so much more confidently than Alice Ambrose was able to in her 1955 paper), that "the state of the philosophy of logic and mathematics . . . gave Wittgenstein good reason to revive the Kantian question 'How is pure mathematics possible?'" (p. 5). Black goes on to make explicit how very deeply indeed Wittgenstein's thought in the *Tractatus* was dominated by Kantian problems. Acknowledging Stenius's contribution here, he goes on to point out with admirable economy and clarity:

Wittgenstein himself saw the analogy when he wrote "Light on Kant's question 'How is pure mathematics possible?' through the theory of tautologies" (*Notebooks*, 15(3) (see also Stenius, *Exposition*, ch. xi: "Wittgenstein as a Kantian philosopher")). Kant in the *Kritik* held our undoubted knowledge of "universal and necessary connexions" in logic and mathematics to be incomprehensible either from the standpoint of Hume's empiricism or from that of Leibniz's rationalism. Wittgenstein would have agreed that if experience is the source of all knowledge, mathematical conclusions ought to be tentative and approximate: while if reason supplies only analytical truth it remains mysterious how mathematics escapes triviality. Pure mathematics cannot be "about" the world in the way that physics is; yet if grounded in thought alone, how can it *apply* to the world? Wittgenstein was absorbed by this ancient puzzle of the connexion between thought and reality: "The great problem round which everything that I write turns is: Is there an order in the world *a priori*, and if so what does it consist in?" (*Notebooks*, 53 (11)). That there must be "an order *in the world*" was a conviction he never abandoned while composing the *Tractatus*; though he came to see that *a priori* propositions "say nothing" he still maintained that in them the "logical form of reality" manifests itself. (Black, pp. 5–6)

Max Black finds other, more specific, Kantian influences in the *Tractatus* as well. The most striking of these is perhaps *Tractatus* 2.013 which reads: "Each thing is, as it were, in a space of possible states of affairs. This space I can imagine empty, but I cannot imagine the thing without the space," and which does indeed seem to be an echo of Kant's point in the *Critique* (A 24 = B 38): "We can never represent to ourselves the absence of space though we can quite well think it as empty of objects." (Black, p. 50).

Maslow's study (3 above) is extremely interesting from our point of view not only because it was the first full-length study to have been written on the *Tractatus*,[5] but also and mainly because it was the first full-scale attempt to unlock its secrets by way of a Kantian interpretation. And that interpretation has since been independently confirmed by Stenius (2 above), whose book (written independently of Maslow's) ends with a chapter entitled "Wittgenstein as a Kantian Philosopher" – a chapter which in a most curious way rediscovers again a good many of the things which Maslow had already discovered in his unpublished study. Not only in this but in many other respects as well, Maslow's study is the most interesting and valuable that we possess. Unfortunately, it is also the most neglected of them.

Maslow tells us in his Introduction[6] that "after several trials, and taking the cue from Russell's Introduction to the *Tractatus*" he has chosen:

> To interpret the book as an inquiry into the formal aspects of means of knowledge, that is, into language or symbolism in general. But I have expanded the meaning and scope of language as universal symbolism so that in my interpretation of the *Tractatus* the basic philosophy underlying it has become a kind of Kantian phenomenalism, with the forms of language playing a role similar to Kant's transcendental apparatus. Language in this interpretation is not only an instrument of thought and communication but also an all-pervading factor in organizing our cognitive experience. (Pp. xiii–xiv)
> (Cf. here Stenius, p. 220: "To sum up: it is essential to Wittgenstein's outlook that logical analysis of language as he conceives of it is a kind of 'transcendental deduction' in Kant's sense, the aim of which is to indicate the *a priori* form of experience which is 'shown' by all meaningful language and therefore cannot be 'said'. From this point of view the *Tractatus* could be called a 'Critique of Pure Language'.")

Very early in his analysis of the *Tractatus*, Maslow raises an objection which might suggest itself to the reader of that work: "It may be said that we are putting the cart before the horse by discussing atomic propositions about facts in order to come to an understanding of the facts themselves – that we seem to decree to reality what features it should possess. In a word we may be accused of dogmatic rationalism the essence of which is the doctrine that reason is the source of real knowledge of the world" (p. 15). To this Maslow replies:

---

[5] Although published only in 1961, it was completed in 1933.
[6] His book contains no index. The following are the page references to Kant: x. xiv, 16, 19, 20, 29, 31–2, 113, 146, 149–50.

The answer to this very serious objection is that we are not making any significant statements about the world, but are discussing the fundamental conditions of all significant symbolism applicable to any world. However, on one hand the formal requirements of symbolism cannot dictate the nature of reality, but on the other hand – and this is of the utmost importance in Wittgenstein's view – we cannot discuss a reality which does not conform to the necessary prerequisite of all symbolism, because we cannot have any discussion (and therefore knowledge) without the medium of symbolism. There is no sense in discussing reality unless it is describable in a language, and it cannot be describable unless its features conform to the formal requirements of all symbolism. We have here a sort of Kantian phenomenalism in Wittgenstein. "Logic is transcendental" (6.13), and the similarity is, I believe, more than merely verbal. (P. 16)

(Cf. here Stenius, p. 218: "We have to realize that what is 'imaginable' and 'intelligible' is what is 'thinkable' and that 'thought' is the 'logical picture of reality,' which means that what is 'thinkable' is that which we can present by a logical picture, or in other words, that which can be *described* in a depicting language. ... Thus to be possible to theoretical reason corresponds in Wittgenstein's philosophy to possibility in terms of what is describable in meaningful language. This is the essential modification of the Kantian view which gives rise to all differences between Wittgenstein and Kant. The *task* of (theoretical) philosophy is for Wittgenstein as for Kant to indicate the limits of theoretical discourse. But since what belongs to theoretical discourse is what can be 'said' at all in language, the investigation of this limit is the investigation of the 'logic' of language, which shows the 'logic of the world.' 'Logic is not a theory but a reflexion of the world,' Wittgenstein says in 6.13, and adds: 'Logic is transcendental,' which can be interpreted in this way: *What Kant's transcendental deductions are intended to perform: this is performed by the logical analysis of language.'*

It would be possible to go on here and show by way of numerous further examples to what remarkably similar conclusions and interpretations both commentators have been led in their independent researches, but to do this properly would take more space than we have here. In Maslow's case these examples and parallels are deeply imbedded in the network of his text and argument as a whole and are difficult to dislodge; in Stenius's case he has devoted a thirteen-page chapter to the topic, one already so highly compressed that it defies further compression.

But let me briefly summarize what we have been able to gather from this review of the existing literature: A good many commentators (including even Stenius) seem to believe that Wittgenstein was not *directly* influenced by Kant but got whatever Kantianism there is to be found in his works from Schopenhauer. Although it will not be my main purpose here to prove whether or not or how much of Kant Wittgenstein read, I believe I shall be able to show in what follows that he certainly must have read surprisingly more of him than has been believed. Secondly, however he got his Kantianism, the existing literature

by its almost total silence regarding its influence on his later workr
seems to imply that it apparently did not extend to it. In what follow,
not only do I hope to show that it did certainly extend to the lates
works as well, but that even as far as the earlier works are concerneds
the influence was of a much more direct and precise nature than has
up till now been supposed (involving as it did, not only such things as a
general and common philosophical orientation, but often even a common
terminology as well). I will begin with the early works.

2

That there is a good deal of Kantianism in Wittgenstein's *Tractatus* no
one I think can doubt after reading Maslow and Stenius. It may, however, be objected that there is much in the *Tractatus* (and especially in
the later works) which have no such antecedents at all. Where, it will
be asked, are such ideas (so distinctive of him) as, for example, that
philosophy is not a body of doctrine but an *activity*; that it is the
logical *clarification* of thought; that it is a kind of *therapy*; that it is a
subject which requires a special kind of *skill* and whose importance lies
in its *method*, etc., where in Kant, it will be asked, are such ideas as
these to be found?

Were these not, after all, the very things whose novelty struck Moore
when he first heard them uttered in Wittgenstein's seminar during
that period of transition between the early and later works? "I was a
good deal surprised," Moore reports of Wittgenstein's lectures, "by some
of the things he said about the difference between 'philosophy' in the
sense in which what he was doing might be called 'philosophy' (he
called this 'modern philosophy'), and what has traditionally been
called 'philosophy.' He said that what he was doing was a 'new
subject,' and not merely a stage in a 'continuous development'; that
there was now, in philosophy, a 'kink' in the 'development of human
thought,' comparable to that which occurred when Galileo and his
contemporaries invented dynamics; that a 'new method' had been
discovered, as has happened when 'chemistry was developed out of
alchemy'; and that it was now possible for the first time that there
should be 'skilful' philosophers, though of course there had in the past
been 'great' philosophers."

"He went on to say that, though philosophy had now been 'reduced
to a matter of skill,' yet this skill, like other skills, is very difficult to

acquire. One difficulty was that it required a 'sort of thinking' to which we are not accustomed and to which we have not been trained – a sort of thinking very different from what is required in the sciences. And he said that the required skill could not be acquired merely by hearing lectures: discussion was essential. As regards his own work, he said it did not matter whether his results were true or not: what mattered was that 'a method had been found'."[7]

Some of these reports refer, of course, to ideas which were only now beginning to ferment in Wittgenstein's mind. There is, however, as more and more readers of Wittgenstein are beginning to see, a good deal more unity and continuity between the early and later works than has hitherto been supposed, these so-called new ideas having their counterparts in the earlier writings.

But regardless whether we call them early or late, where, the question is, are they indeed to be found if not in Wittgenstein alone? I believe we can say that although these ideas seem new and original, they are not without their historical antecedents. I believe we can even say that not only was Wittgenstein mistaken in thinking that he was breaking entirely new ground here, he was also mistaken in thinking that he was breaking it in the entirely new way he thought he was. For, interestingly enough, such ideas are to be found in Kant as well. My source is Kant's Introduction to his *Logic*[8] – a much neglected work but one whose contents deserve close attention.

The first section of this work deals with the problem of the nature of Logic. Logic, he says here, is concerned with the rules of the operation of the understanding in general – rules which are absolutely necessary to it and which are totally independent of objects or any knowledge we may borrow from them. "The science," he says, "which contains these universal and necessary laws is simply a science of the form of thought. And we can form a conception of the possibility of such a science, just as of a *universal grammar* which contains nothing beyond the mere form of language, without words, which belong to the matter of language."[9]

Some logicians, however, have misunderstood its nature and have introduced some false principles and materials in its study.[10]

Some logicians, indeed, presuppose in Logic *psychological* principles. But it	Psychology is no more closely related to philosophy than any other natural

---

[7] *Philosophical Papers*, (New York: Collier Books, 1962), pp. 315–16.
[8] *Kant's Introduction to Logic*, tr. T. K. Abbott, (New York: Philosophical Library, 1963).
[9] P. 2.
[10] *The Chief Works of Benedict De Spinoza*, tr. R. H. M. Elwes, (New York: Dover Publications, Inc., 1951), Vol. II, p. 74.

is just as inappropriate to bring principles of this kind into Logic as to derive the science of morals from life. If we were to take the principles from psychology, that is, from observations on our understanding, we should merely see *how* thought takes place, and *how* it is affected by the manifold subjective hindrances and conditions; so that this would lead only to the knowledge of *contingent* laws. But in Logic the question is not of *contingent*, but of *necessary* laws; not how we do think, but how we ought to think. The rules of Logic, then, must not be derived from the *contingent*, but from the *necessary* use of the understanding, which, without any psychology, a man finds in himself. In Logic we do not want to know how the understanding is and thinks, and how it has hitherto proceeded in thinking, but how it ought to proceed in thinking. Its business is to teach us the correct use of reason, that is, the use which is consistent with itself. (P. 4)

science. Theory of knowledge is the philosophy of psychology. Does not my study of sign-language correspond to the study of thought-processes, which philosophers used to consider so essential to the philosophy of logic? Only in most cases they got entangled in unessential psychological investigations, and with my method too there is an analogous risk. (*Tractatus* 4.1121). In logic nothing is accidental. (*Tractatus* 2.012). The person who is calculating in my language-game does not think of it as a peculiarity of *his* nature that he gets *this*; the fact does not appear to him as a psychological one. (*Remarks on the Foundations of Mathematics*, tr. G. E. M. Anscombe. Oxford: Basil Blackwell, 1956, p. 162).

Logic, however, Kant continues, may be divided into two parts: Analytic and Dialectic. While Analytic Logic deals with the formal rules or criteria of truth, Dialectic Logic deals with the ways in which the untrue may be given the appearance or may be made to appear as true. This is not how Dialectic has been conceived in the past. It used to be thought of and cultivated by Greek dialecticians as the art of semblance (going under the name, the Art of Disputation) – an art devoted to teaching how to deceive by way of semblance.

But nothing can be more unworthy of a philosopher than the cultivation of such an art. It must therefore be altogether dropped in this aspect of it, and instead of it there must be introduced into Logic a critical examination of this semblance. We should therefore have two parts of Logic; the *Analytic*, which should treat of the formal criteria of truth, and the *Dialectic*, which should contain the marks and rules by which we should be able to know that something does not agree with the formal criteria of truth, although it seems to

My aim is: to teach you to pass from a piece of disguised nonsense to something that is patent nonsense. (*Philosophical Investigations*, tr. G. E. M. Anscombe. Oxford: Basil Blackwell, 1953, I, 109). The philosopher is the man who has to cure himself of many sicknesses of the understanding before he can arrive at the notions of the sound human understanding. (*R.F.M.*, p. 157). The philosopher's treatment of a question is like the treatment of an illness. (*P.I.*, I, 225). There is not *a* philosophical method, though there

agree with them. Dialectic in this as-
spect would have its use as a *Cathartic*
of the understanding. (P. 7)

are indeed methods, like therapies.
(*P.I.*, I, 133).

Continuing with what Logic is and what it is not, we must note, Kant
says, that it is neither a "general Art of Discovery, nor an Organon of
Truth"; it is also not "an Algebra, by help of which hidden truths may
be discovered."

Nevertheless it is useful and indispensable as a *criticism of knowledge*; or
for passing judgment on the common,
as well as the speculative reason, not
for the purpose of teaching it, but in
order to make it *correct* and consistent
with itself. (P. 10). It is the business of
Logic *to make clear concepts distinct.*
(P. 53). But ... by this, which is
mere analysis, my knowledge is not
increased as to its comprehension.
This remains the same; only the form
is changed, inasmuch as what already
was contained in the given concept
I now learn to distinguish better, or to
recognize with clear consciousness.
Just as by mere illumination of a
map nothing is added to it, so by
the mere clearing up of a given concept
by analysis of its attributes this concept itself is not in the least degree
enlarged. ... The philosopher only
makes given concepts distinct. (P. 54).

All philosophy is a "critique of
language." (*Tractatus* 4.0031). Philosophy aims at the logical clarification
of thoughts. ... Without philosophy
thoughts are, as it were, cloudy and
indistinct: its task is to make them
clear and to give them sharp boundaries. (*Tractatus* 4.112). He sees a way
of dividing the county different from
the one used on the ordinary map. (*The
Blue and Brown Books*, p. 57). We must
do away with all *explanation*, and description alone must take its place. And
this description gets its power of illumination – i.e., its purpose – from the
philosophical problems. These are, of
course, not empirical problems ... the
problems are solved, not by giving new
information, but by arranging what we
have always known. (*P.I.*, I, 109). It is
... of the essence of our investigation
that we do not seek to learn anything
new by it. We want to *understand* something that is already in plain view.
(*P.I.*, I, 89).

Having defined the nature of Logic, Kant moves on to the conception
of philosophy itself. There is, he writes, what we might call scholastic
philosophy and cosmic philosophy – one appeals to *skill*, the other to
wisdom. Both, however, are required in a philosopher.

According to the *cosmic conception* of
it, is the science of the ultimate ends
of human reason. This high conception
gives *dignity* to philosophy, that is, an
absolute value, and which first gives
value to all other branches of knowledge. (p. 14) Philosophy, in the
scholastic conception of it, includes...
a sufficient stock of rational knowledge
and ... a systematic connexion of the
parts of this knowledge, or a combination of them into the idea of a whole.

It has been what I should like to call
my strong scholastic feeling that has
occasioned my best discoveries. (*Notebooks 1914–16*, tr. G. E. M. Anscombe.
Oxford: Basil Blackwell, 1961, p. 28).
Where does our investigation get its
importance from, since it seems only
to destroy everything interesting,
that is, all that is great and important?
(As it were all the buildings, leaving
behind only bits of stone and rubble.)
What we are destroying is nothing

(P. 15) In the scholastic signification of the word, philosophy aims only at *skill*; in reference to the higher or cosmic conception, on the contrary, it aims at *utility*. (P. 14) Both must be united. (P. 16) No one can call himself a philosopher who cannot philosophize. ... It is only by practice and independent use of one's reason that one can learn to philosophize. How, indeed can Philosophy be learned? Every philosophical thinker builds his own work on the ruins, so to speak, of another; but nothing has ever been built that could be permanent in all its parts. It is, therefore, impossible to learn philosophy, even for this reason that it *does not yet exist*. (P. 16) We must, therefore, for the sake of exercize in independent thought or philosophizing, look more to the *method* of employment of reason than to the propositions themselves, at which we have arrived by its means. (P. 17)

but houses of cards and we are clearing up the ground of language on which they stand. (*P.I.*, I, 118.) Philosophy is not one of the natural sciences. (The word "philosophy" must mean something whose place is above or below the natural sciences, not beside them.) ... Philosophy is not a body of doctrine but an activity. A philosophic work consists essentially of elucidations. Philosophy does not result in "philosophical propositions," but rather in the clarification of propositions. (*Tractatus* 4.111–4.112.) I was a good deal surprised by some of the things he said about the difference between "philosophy" (he called this "modern philosophy"), and what has traditionally been called "philosophy." He said that what he was doing was a "new subject" ... that a "new method" had been discovered ... that that it was now possible for the first time that there should be "skilful" philosophers, though of course there had in the past been "great" philosophers. (Moore's Notes.)

I believe it is impossible to read these various passages from Kant's Introduction to the *Logic* without, it seems to be, becoming intensely aware of the curious impact which they seemed to have had upon Wittgenstein. Certainly in some cases he himself was not unaware of this effect, as is clear, for example, from Mays's report noted above that he "likened himself to Kant" in emphasizing "that philosophy was an activity rather than a subject." But above all these references and parallels make clear that Wittgenstein had obviously read much more of Kant than has been supposed and read him much more closely too.

3

These references and parallels with Kant's *Logic*, although valuable and interesting in themselves, tend to raise also, however, a number of questions regarding Wittgenstein's early metaphysical (or "cosmic") beliefs. Since what can be said of this subject is connected in an interesting way with his later views and writings (especially with the kind of expression he chose for them) it might be well to spend some moments on them.

Now what is so significant, from this point of view, about the various passages from the *Logic* considered above is that they enable us to see a good deal better just what were the nature of the limits within which Wittgenstein apparently decided to pursue his own studies. As the passages above seem to reveal, had he followed Kant a little more close-ly these would normally not have included that vast area of speculation which Kant entitled "cosmic" philosophy and which some people now-adays like to call "the nonsensical." But as it was he did not follow him that closely. On the other hand, by their very nature they could not but affect his attitude to what lay beyond these limits.

There has been a great deal of discussion regarding these limits and especially of Wittgenstein's ambivalent attitude to what is supposed to lie beyond them. It has also been said that his attitude in this respect had undergone a change. In a sense this is true. This change, however, does not lie entirely in the direction in which it has generally been conceived, for even in the *Tractatus* period there were obviously for him things concerning which we must, he felt, be silent. But although Wittgenstein's reasons for believing this are well known, there is one which he gives in the *Philosophical Investigations* which seems to have gone unnoticed, and which does represent, or would represent, a funda-mental change in attitude. The passage that I have in mind is I, 128: "If one tried to advance *theses* in philosophy," he says there, "it would never be possible to question them, because everyone would agree to them." I do not wish to make too much of one quotation but what it seems to suggest to me is that perhaps one of the reasons why he came finally to abandon "cosmic" philosophy for the sort which requires only "skill," was not because he felt that the attempt to deal with such things necessarily reduces one to speak nonsense or that language must be strained in order to do so, but rather because, like Leonard Nelson before him, he came to see that that kind of philosophy was simply not subject to controversy and that therefore nothing very much could be said about it.

This implies, of course, that Wittgenstein had, at one point at least, subscribed to a kind of "cosmic" philosophy, and the question is, What sort of philosophy or metaphysics was that? That is not a difficult question to answer, for all the evidence seems to suggest that the main influence upon him during this early period was Spinoza. How very much, in fact, Wittgenstein was intoxicated with Spinoza is apparent from the *Notebooks* and the *Tractatus*, whole sections of which speak eloquently of it (including, in the case of the *Tractatus*, its "geometrical" design).

The very lovely and moving lines in the *Notebooks*, with their interesting rhythmic parallels to the well-known and famous lines from Spinoza's Appendix to Part I of the *Ethics* come immediately to mind here.

"In the foregoing I have explained," Spinoza's passage begins, "the nature and properties of God."

"I have shown that he necessarily exists, that he is one: that he is, and acts solely by the necessity of his own nature; that he is the free cause of all things, and how he is so; that all things are in God, and so depend on him, that without him they could neither exist nor be conceived; lastly, that all things are predetermined by God, not through his free will or absolute fiat, but from the very nature of God or infinite power."

Wittgenstein's is:

What do I know about God and the purpose of life?
I know that this world exists.
That I am placed in it like my eye in its visual field.
That something about it is problematic, which we call its meaning.
That this meaning does not lie in it but outside it.
That life is the world.
That my will penetrates the world.
That my will is good or evil.
Therefore that good and evil are somehow connected with the meaning of the world.
The meaning of life, i.e., the meaning of the world, we can call God.
And connect with this the comparison of God to a father.
To pray is to think about the meaning of life.
I cannot bend the happenings of the world to my will: I am completely powerless.
I can only make myself independent of the world – and so in a certain sense master it – by renouncing any influence on happenings.[11]

These lines are dated 11.6.16. A little later the same year he asks himself this question: "But is it possible for one so to live that life stops being problematic? That one is *living* in eternity and not in time?"[12]

[11] *Notebooks*, pp. 72–3.
[12] P. 74.

And he answers: "In order to live happily I must be in agreement with the world. And that is what "being happy" *means*."[13] With Spinoza again clearly in mind, he remarks: "the world in itself is neither good for evil";[14] "good and evil only enter through the *subject*."[15] In the same vein and using again almost the same words that Spinoza had used, he writes: "There cannot be an orderly or a disorderly world, so that one could say that our world is orderly."[16] Combining, finally, the insights of Schopenhauer with those of Spinoza, he notes: "The work of art is the object seen *sub specie aeternitatis*; and the good life is the world seen *sub specie aeternitatis*. This is the connexion between art and ethics."[17]

If this was the kind of "cosmic" philosophy which Wittgenstein later came to abandon (assuming he ever did abandon it), I think it would be a mistake to believe that he did so abruptly. On the contrary, the transition seems to have been both an orderly and a subtle one, and not without its Kantian overtones and connexions. For this Spinoza interest, so intense in the early works, does not stop at the *Philosophical Investigations* – a work in which he carries on, as one might perhaps describe it, a kind of dialogue with himself for "cathartic" or therapeutic purposes. On the contrary, in that work too he shows evidence of still being very much under the domination (as Freud was before him) of Spinoza's thought, and especially its main psychological principle. For it was, after all, the argument of Freud, and it is similarly the argument of Wittgenstein, that the objects of their respective studies will cease to have the hold on us that they have and will cease to

---

[13] P. 75.

[14] P. 79.

[15] *Ibid.*

[16] P. 83. Cf. here Spinoza's Appendix to Part I of the *Ethics*, p. 79: "... inasmuch as those who do not understand the nature of things do not verify phenomena in any way, but merely imagine them after a fashion, and mistake their imagination for understanding, such persons firmly believe that there is an *order* in things, being really ignorant both of things and their own nature. When phenomena are of such a kind, that the impression they make on our senses require little effort of imagination, and can consequently be easily remembered, we say that they are *well-ordered*; if the contrary, that they are *ill-ordered* or confused. ... as though there were any order in nature except in relating to our imagination ..." In view of such (and many other) striking parallels, it is surprising that so little has been said about Wittgenstein's relation to Spinoza. References to Spinoza in books on Wittgenstein are, in fact, rare. A noted exception is Professor Max Black's book, *A Companion to Wittgenstein's "Tractatus"*.

[17] *Notebooks*, p. 83. This mixture of Schopenhauerian and Spinozist themes is characteristic not only of a good many other notes in this collection, but also of some of the propositions (e.g., those from 6.61 to 6.45) in the *Tractatus*. His attempt to bring Spinoza's theory of psycho-physical parallelism into harmony with some of Schopenhauer's biological theories from Schopenhauer's *Will in Nature* in his observations dated 15.10.16 (pp. 84–5) are especially interesting.

"trouble" us once we gain an insight into their source and origin. Even a philosophy of "skill" is not, thus, to use the language of Kant's *Logic*, without its "utility" either.

But here also perhaps too much ought not to be made of this no doubt interesting point. On the other hand, however, it is extremely revealing to read some of Wittgenstein's later works in the light of this psychological principle of Spinoza. Combined in his mind, as I believe it became, with his observations of Kant's doctrines regarding the logic of our mental operations, it became the guiding thread of his own investigations and the occasion for expressing them in the clinical terms so distinctive of them.[18]

It is to Kant's analysis of the logic of these mental operations that I should now like to turn.

4

Parallels between Wittgenstein's *Tractatus* and some of Kant's basic ideas have not been, relatively speaking, difficult to trace. It is perhaps not even surprising that his readers were so very quickly able to sense their presence. On the other hand, the parallels between Kant's Introduction to his *Logic* and some of Wittgenstein's ideas, which I have tried to trace above, have generally gone unnoticed because that work of Kant's is seldom any longer studied or read.

The parallels to which I should now like to draw the reader's attention are even of a more surprising nature. They have to do with what is probably the main thesis of Wittgenstein's *Philosophical Investigations*, the thesis, that is, regarding the way in which we are led astray "by means of language."

There are two goals I have in mind in pursuing this particular investigation. First of all, I should like to be able to show that this seemingly new and revolutionary idea is also not without its philo-

---

[18] In a sense, however, this was something of a retrogressive step. For by reducing the problems of epistemology into purely logical terms, Kant had set that discipline on a firm basis, advancing it enormously. In fact one might even say that Kant was the first person to achieve a distinct view of that science. For Descartes still finds it necessary to speak of *vital spirits*, Spinoza of *peace of mind*, Locke of the *genesis of ideas*, and Hume of *habits*. In Kant all such psychological considerations fall away, the problems emerging at last pure and unmixed. Seen from this point of view, Wittgenstein's tendency to discuss these problems in clinical terms – understandable though this is in view of the time in which he wrote – is nevertheless in a way unfortunate. The same, of course, is not true of his reduction of these problems to linguistic or grammatical terms. See, however, my discussion in the final chapter of this work.

sophical and historical antecedents. Secondly, and more importantly, I believe this doctrine of Wittgenstein's has not been fully understood. Seeing it in its historical context may perhaps enable us to see better just what it was meant to convey.

Let me then proceed to outline Kant's argument, throwing into relief those aspects of it which are mutually illuminating and which bear directly upon Wittgenstein's linguistic thesis.

Now like the Wittgensteinian philosophy, not the least remarkable feature of Kant's *Critique of Pure Reason* is its claim to have brought about a number of original, profound, and lasting revolutions. Yet in outline the work is not unlike (strangely enough perhaps) many other great metaphysical classics. For the main problem of the *Critique* is whether we have any justification for our belief in God, freedom and immortality, and although the argument consists of an intricate and searching analysis of the limits of knowledge and the reach of science and only comes to deal with the question of our knowledge of God when that analysis has been completed, the hope of achieving some satisfying answer to this problem lies behind and inspires the whole undertaking. Despite its revolutionary claims, therefore, the *Critique of Pure Reason* lies very much within the great stream of philosophic speculation.

Within the great stream, however, Kant's thought is distinguished, again, not unlike Wittgenstein's, by its freedom from dogma and remorseless self-examination. His age, Kant said, was an age of criticism, and to criticism everything must submit. Neither religion nor morals can claim exemption from it, nor need they fear it; for if it is not within our powers, as he remarked, ever firmly to establish those truths or propositions which most concern us, neither can it ever be in anyone's power to destroy the foundations upon which they rest. For where is such knowledge to come from? If they cannot be confirmed, neither can they be refuted. On the contrary, freedom of inquiry, he said, should be encouraged, even provoked, for "the root of these disturbances, which lies deep in the nature of human reason, must be removed. But how can we do so, unless we give it freedom, nay, nourishment, to send out shoots so that it may discover itself to our eyes, and that it may then be entirely destroyed?"[19] His own experience in these matters led him to expect much from such practices, and he invited others to follow his example. "Whenever I hear that a writer of real ability has demonstrated away the freedom of the human will, the hope of a future life, and the

---

[19] *Immanuel Kant's Critique of Pure Reason*, tr. Norman Kemp Smith, (London: Macmillan & Co., 1953), p. 618 (A 778 = B 806).

existence of God," he declared in this connexion, "I am eager to read the book, for I expect him by his talents to increase my insight into these matters. ... The reply of the *dogmatic* defender of the good cause I should not read at all."[20] On the other hand, indifference to such metaphysical questions was not, he felt, compatible with being human.

Some disturbances could not be so easily uprooted. (It is, in most cases, impossible to show an exact point where an analogy begins to mislead us. *B.B.*, p. 28). He made this discovery when he tried to resolve certain conflicts of a particularly aggravating nature, which he called "antinomies of reason." To deal with them at all required, he soon came to realize, a complete investigation of our whole faculty of knowledge to see what was and what was not in our power to know. What puzzled him about these old dilemmas was not the *facts* which they purported to describe but their description which in each case gave rise to pairs of contradictory propositions neither of which could be denied without absurdity. (Our problem is not a causal but a conceptual one. *P.I.*, II, xi; The puzzlement about the grammar of the word "time" arises from what one might call apparent contradictions in that grammar. *B.B.*, p. 26). The more he reflected upon this curious situation into which reason seemed to have gotten herself, the more certain he became that some quite natural and inevitable illusion ("... which can no more be prevented than we can prevent the sea from appearing higher at the horizon than at the shore ...")[21] lay behind it. He was fascinated by this aberration of reason and was intent upon uncovering its peculiar transcendental illusion. "The year 1769," he later recorded with gratitude, "brought me great light." He had reason to be grateful, for it was in that light that the *Critique of Pure Reason* was born.

The four antinomies which he brings forward in the *Critique*, examples of the sort of question which human reason is *fated* to ask but not fit to answer, exhibit this restlessness and self-contradiction of reason. The first centres round the ancient conflict whether the world has a beginning in Time and an end in Space, and proceeds in the following fashion.

In regard to Time, so the advocates of the Thesis argue, the world must be finite, for at any given moment in its history it is possible to say that the series of past events up to that moment have come to an end and been completed, but if the world has (as the advocates of the

[20] P. 602 (A 753 = B 781).
[21] P. 299 (A 297 = B 354). Cf. here *P.I.*, I, 109–115.

Antithesis claim) no beginning, then what has passed by and been completed was what in the nature of the case could neither have passed by nor been completed, namely, an eternity and infinity of past events. We are therefore compelled to say that the world had a beginning in Time.

Similarly with the infinity of the world in Space. If the world has no limits in Space then it must be an infinite whole which would require an infinite time to traverse, but a whole which requires an infinite to traverse can never be traversed, and therefore there shall never come a time when we shall be able to say of the world as a whole that it is infinite in Space. Such a statement would be self-negating, for to make it at any one particular time would mean to bring the infinite to an end at the very moment when we are maintaining that it is infinite, i.e., that it has no end.

But if the world had a beginning in Time, the advocates of the Antithesis can reply with equal cogency, then there must have been a time when there was no time, yet still a time when the world arose, which is absurd. The world therefore must be conceived as having no beginning. Similarly with the infinity of the world in Space. If the world is limited in Space then it is limited by something which is nothing, which is equally absurd and self-negating. The world therefore must be conceived as being infinite in Space as well.

But the world *must* be finite, for at any given moment in its history it is possible to say that the series of past events up to that moment have come to an end and been completed, but if the world has no beginning, then ... and so, on and on it goes.

Obviously there can be no end to this argument, for no one assertion is superior to another and the only victor is he who is permitted to say the last word.

These antinomies, Kant says, are symptomatic of and represent reason's proud pretensions to a kind of knowledge to which it can never attain. Yet reason's great expectations in the realm of the Infinite are expressive of some very deep human needs and deal with questions (were they but answerable) which far surpass in dignity and importance all other human science. This may not be immediately apparent from the dry formulas in which they have thus far been represented, but only a little imagination is required in order to see them in their true light and full splendor. For whether the world has a beginning in Time and an end in Space; whether the self is indivisible and indestructible or merely transitory and perishable; whether man is free or is a creature of fate or nature; whether, finally, there is a supreme cause of the world – these are questions for the solution of which, he declares in a burst of eloquence, the mathematician would gladly exchange the whole of his science, yet they are ones which every right-thinking person must ask himself if he has any understanding of what truly concerns him. Indifference to these matters is out of the question, for both our honor and rationality are at stake and it is not possible to withdraw from the conflict without doing irreparable damage to both. Rather we must see whether some misunderstanding lies at the root of these conflicts, the resolution of which may provide the way for a "lasting and peaceful reign of reason over understanding and the senses."[22] (The real discovery is the one that makes me capable of stopping doing philosophy when I want to. – The one that gives philosophy peace, so that it is no longer tormented by questions which bring *itself* in question. (*P.I.*, I, 133).

If for the moment we were to defer the question of truth and consider merely the question of motives we would see at once why some, though not influenced by any superior insight into the matter under dispute, have preferred to fight on one side rather than on the other, and why the one side conducts its campaign with passionate zeal supported by the noisy approval of its countless sympathizers, while the other proceeds with calm assurance but in an atmosphere of mistrust and prejudice. For two diverse systems of philosophy are in conflict here, empiricism and rationalism, and each is driven to maintain its position by powerful and pressing needs. For rationalism these needs are best served by the theses of the argument whose propositions are the foundation stones of morals and religion. Empiricism, whose own interests are deeply bound up with the antitheses, by denying that we shall ever achieve final answers to the problems of religion and natural science – by denying, that is to say, that the world has a beginning, that the soul is immortal, that man is free, and that God exists – robs us, or seems to rob us, of all these moral and intellectual supports. It is not surprising, therefore, that the rationalist position, which satisfies our deep and natural craving for a "finished" universe (in which alone our reason can find comfort and come to rest) should generate so much respect and command such a great following. (What makes it difficult for us to take this line of investigation is our craving for generality ... completeness. ... This tendency is the real source of metaphysics, and leads the philosopher into complete darkness. *B.B.*, pp. 17–19.)

[22] P. 423 (A 465 = B 493).

But that respect, Kant warns the reader, is as much unearned as the mistrust and prejudice, for the satisfaction which supports it is based upon an illusion which, ultimately, can bring comfort to no one. Such knowledge as we desire, sad and comfortless as this no doubt is, will always be out of our reach – however much we may desire it.

We can, however, come to understand why it is we desire it. (There is a tendency rooted in our usual forms of expression. *B.B.*, p. 17; the logic of language ... seduces us ... *P.I.*, I, 93.) Put very simply, it is this.

It is the function of the Understanding to absorb, unify and organize all the material that falls within its orbit. This it does in certain prescribed ways made familiar to us by Logic. Logic, it is true, cannot tell us what we shall think or experience, but as the science of the laws of thought it does decide how we shall think and experience it. (To give the essence of a proposition means to give the essence of all description, and thus the essence of the world. *Tractatus* 5.4711; Grammar tells what kind of object anything is. *P.I.*, I, 373.) In a very real sense, therefore, what we can come to know about the world is determined in advance by the nature of our Understanding. It is for this reason that we can know, for example, that the Principle of Causation will always characterize the world of our experience, for one of the logical principles which governs our thought is that of implication, and although "implication" (the ground-consequent relation) is not "causation" (the cause-effect relation), being however fundamental and isomorphic with it, we can be certain that the mind's determination to organize its experience in this way will never be frustrated. For all theoretical and practical purposes, we are therefore justified in assuming that the Concept of Causation has objective validity. And so it is with all the other logical, scientific concepts.

But the Understanding is not the only faculty of knowledge. Its domain is the world of sense which it organizes and unifies according to its various Categories or Concepts, ultimately derived, as we have seen, from Logic. But above it, and paralleling its function, is Reason, whose domain is the world of Categories itself, which it, in turn, organizes and unifies by principles – or "Ideas" – no less compelling, and whose ultimate source too is Logic. This it does by means of the Syllogism which is Reason's unique tool and is as much a part of its nature as the Proposition (whose structure, according to Kant, corresponds to the structure of the world) out of which it is compounded. But unlike, now, the Proposition, which has a beginning and an end (and which issues in a Concept having objective validity), a Syllogism is, so to speak, un-bounded and incomplete, and the Idea (a First Cause, God, etc.) which issues from it no longer has any such objective validity. On the other hand the nature of *its* structure (no less than the structure of the Propo-sition) is such that Reason is necessarily led to think that such an objective correlative does indeed exist. (We are led into puzzlement by an analogy which irresistibly drags us on. *B.B.*, p. 108; You interpret a grammatical movement made by yourself as a quasi-physical phe-nomenon which you are observing. *P.I.*, I, 401.) Urged on and domi-nated by the requirements of its own nature, Reason – all too naturally – snatches at it and posits it.

Almost any syllogism can serve as an illustration of this tyranny which Reason exercises over the Understanding. Thus – to take an example – in the syllogism:

> All men are mortal
> All scholars are men
> All scholars are mortal

the conclusion, we are driven to see, rests and is derived from a premise (All men are mortal) which is merely the conclusion of another syllogism – its somewhat more embracing pro-syllogism, *viz.*

> All animals are mortal
> All men are animals
> All men are mortal

But, obviously, we cannot rest here either, for this conclusion now is in its turn dependent upon a premise (All animals are mortal) which is simply the conclusion of a still more fundamental pro-pro-syllogism. Nor will our search come to an end there, for its conclusion is, again, dependent upon a premise, itself dependent upon a conclusion, resting again upon a premise, whose conclusion in turn is based, etc., etc. (The man who is philosophically puzzled sees a law in the way a word is used, and, trying to apply this law consistently, comes up against cases where it leads to paradoxical results. *B.B.*, p. 27.)

To this infinite series of regressions there is of course no end, but Reason deeply committed to its search, and ever assured of its nearness, reaches for it and asserts it. Such an End, it thinks, must necessarily exist, absolutely necessary, as it is, to think it. (We think it must be in reality; for we think we already see it there. *P.I.*, I, 101.) Thus it is that "in all peoples, there shine amidst the most benighted polytheism some gleams of monotheism, to which they have been led, not by reflection and profound speculation, but simply by the natural bent of the common understanding, as step by step it has come to apprehend its own requirements."[23] (Thus it can come about that we aren't able to rid ourselves of the implications of our symbolism. *B.B.*, p. 108.)

Still, as it has often been pointed out, certitude is no test of certainty, and the Idea of such an End or Supreme Cause must forever remain what it is – simply an Idea, a thought, an illusion.

But these hopes and illusions are not ones which can ever be eradicated from the mind, however harmless we may succeed in rendering them. And that is not possible, for the anomaly from which Reason here suffers is not, so to speak, a *personal* one, and therefore not amenable to that kind of treatment. Nor, of course, is it an *anomaly*. The supposition that it is, the supposition that the errors of Reason here are somehow due to some "fault of its own" and therefore is to be treated in the manner, say, of Locke's "*physiology* of the human understanding," is precisely what[24] makes Locke's experiment with the historical, plain method such an outstanding failure. (It is not a stupid prejudice. *P.I.*, I, 340; The problems arising through a misinterpretation of our forms of language have the character of depth. They are deep disquietudes. *P.I.*, I, 111.)

This is, if I understand it correctly, Kant's teaching regarding the problem of our will to metaphysics.

It is also, as I have tried to indicate in the course of this summary, and as I now wish to go on to explain further, what seems to underly Wittgenstein's own thought on these matters – especially concerning what it is that lies behind such striking but dark and obscure clinical phrases as "grammatical illusion," "urge to misunderstand," "bewitchment," and so on, which otherwise seem, I think, so puzzling and so curiously lacking in content.

5

The parallels which I have tried to draw the reader's attention to above, do not only enable us, I think to see more clearly the kind of content Wittgenstein meant to pack into these curious and dark phrases, they also enable us to see better or state more clearly the very serious objection to which they give rise.

[23] P. 499 (A 590 = B 618).
[24] As he points out in the Preface to the First Edition of the *Critique*. See p. 7 and p. 8 (A vii and A ix).

Let me turn first to the nature of the clue these parallels provide for this deeper understanding of his linguistic doctrine.

It seems to me that having come in contact with Kant's thought and feeling that Kant had gone very far in making clear the nature of the mind's operations, Wittgenstein saw that it was possible to put these insights of Kant in a new way, and to throw a completely new light on them – in fact that they had or could have an altogether different application. From Kant he had learned, as I have tried to point out above, that the *forms of judgment* determine, in a way that had never been suspected before, the various lines and patterns of our thought, creating in the process our various hopes and illusions. It suddenly dawned on him that what Kant had taught applied to language itself. He had already undertaken this sort of reduction (as I will point out again below) in the *Tractatus* and so he now systematically substituted *forms of expression* for Kant's forms of judgment. The result must have seemed enormously exciting. The problem of Kant's *Critique* was why people have thought that they had the kind of knowledge, or had such an intense urge to possess the kind of knowledge, which in his view they could not possibly obtain or satisfy. As a result of his researches Kant came to see that what impelled them to it was Reason's tyranny over the Understanding, driving it to seek completeness and a "finished" universe, one having a beginning in Time, and an end in Space, etc. And it was the same with Wittgenstein. The prejudices which stand in the way of our seeing how words are actually used, are not, he came to see, "*stupid* prejudices." On the contrary, they have the "character of depth" and are symptomatic of "deep disquietudes" – for their source is, as he too came to put it, "our craving for generality," for "completeness." It is this which "bewitches" the mind, gives rise to "grammatical illusions" and "urges" it to grasp and embrace matters which are ultimately simply a product of our own making. Putting this more concretely and translating it into more nearly linguistic terms, what Wittgenstein came to see was that philosophical puzzlement arose from our desire to see and introduce into language more consistency and neatness than actually exist in it, or which it can accomodate. "The man who is philosophically puzzled," as he put it, "sees a law in the way a word is used and, trying to apply this law consistently, comes up against cases where it leads to paradoxical results." (*B.B.*, p. 27.) To surmount these results, we must therefore "fight against the fascination which forms of expression exert upon us." (*Ibid.*)

The trouble was, however, that while the Kantian formulation of the doctrine, dealing as it did, with some of the fundamental patterns of our thought, carried a conviction which is strikingly forceful, by reducing the problem in the way he now did, it became extremely difficult to show why we should have become saddled with such curious desires. It is a kind of difficulty or objection which every reader of Wittgenstein has felt. What precisely is it about language, one is always tempted to ask, which manages to exercise such a tyranically bewitching power over our minds, one that apparently enables it to continue to deceive us even when its deceptions are brought to light and exposed. What seem so especially puzzling about the theory is its emphasis upon this sense of doom and inevitability. For Wittgenstein's argument is not simply that philosophers have been led into confusion "by means of language"; it is that (language being what it is) they have been irresistibly and forcibly led into it. But Wittgenstein's diagnosis here has seemed to many (to Lazerowitz, for example, as we saw above) too simple, too incredible, too absurd. If language truly doomed philosophers to speak nonsense, the doom they have been inclined to object, must be sealed at a level deeper than the strictly linguistic one. And, strangely enough, Wittgenstein's clinical phrases seemed to allow for – even point to – such a deeper level. The parallel with Kant makes it clear what that level was perhaps meant to be.

But although the parallel is, I believe, close and makes Wittgenstein's analysis more understandable, it does not succeed in making his doctrine entirely persuasive. For if we compare, for example, Kant's analysis of how the mind comes to its conception of God (nay, cannot avoid coming to it) with Wittgenstein's analysis of, for example, how we come to our false expectation (which we can, I believe, easily avoid) regarding the measurability of Time, we see immediately that while the Kantian formulation, dealing as it does with some of the fundamental internal patterns of our thought, carries conviction, Wittgenstein's reduction or translation, depending as it does on seemingly external and contingent factors, does not. What Wittgenstein's analysis, in other words, seems to lack is precisely this element of universality and inevitability that is such a convincing part of Kant's doctrine and analysis. For after all, with Kant it is not a matter of any one particular syllogism leading us to draw an invalid inference. His doctrine of transcendental illusions is not derived in any such way; on the contrary, any syllogism at all could serve as an illustration, for it is the *form* of the syllogism (expressive as that is of the pattern of our thought) which gives rise to such illusions and not its matter. No particular example need therefore be especially defended or regarded as preeminent – some universal feature concerning the operation of our minds guarantees that the facts are as stated, and inevitably so.

But in Wittgenstein the matter seems entirely reversed. His dialectic, which lacks this kind of built-in guarantee or transcendentalism, seems always in need of further and further support, each time requiring to be proven anew. His examples, as a result, assume enormous importance, each becoming a kind of test-case of his entire argument.

Wittgenstein was not, I believe, unaware of this gap, one which seemed to threaten his whole structure of thought. To close this gap a bridge was needed. The *Blue Book* testifies to his urgent search for such a bridge. I will argue in my next chapter that Wittgenstein found what he thought he needed here in the linguistic writings of Schopenhauer. That he felt uneasy about this linguistic solution, however, is I believe indicated by the numerous warnings he felt it necessary to give there regarding the use of his new "method": "The idea of an analogy being misleading," he remarks at one point, "is nothing sharply defined." (*B.B.*, p. 28.) "It is, in most cases," he urges at another, "impossible to show an exact point where an analogy begins to mislead us." (*Ibid.*) This, of course, did not prevent him from introducing various examples of his own, but, revealingly enough, these tend to diminish drastically in the subsequent writings, and it is probably not too much to say that none of them ever pleased him entirely. In the nature of the case, of course, none could.

I do not wish to imply that what I have written here actually passed before Wittgenstein's mind. Perhaps none of it did. But seen in this way, it becomes clear what, I believe, the content of such dark and puzzling phrases as "grammatical illusion," "bewilderment," "craving for generality," "urgue to misunderstand," "depth grammar," "bewitchment," "spell," "troubles," "delusion," and so on were meant to convey.

Now it might be thought that this idea of translating these Kantian insights into purely linguistic terms came only late and suddenly to Wittgenstein. I think that to think so would be a mistake. The idea of such a reconstruction seems, on the contrary, to have occurred to him very early in his career as a philosopher. This is shown by the *Tractatus* (to return once more to that work) where it is already, I believe, at work.

The *Tractatus* deals, he says of it in his Preface, "with the problems of philosophy, and shows, I believe, that the reason why these problems are posed is that the logic of our language is misunderstood. The whole

sense of the book might be summed up in the following words: what can
be said at all can be said clearly, and what we cannot talk about we
must consign to silence."

"Thus the aim of the book is to set a limit to thought, or rather – not
to thought, but to the *expression* of thoughts: for in order to be able
to set a limit to thought, we should have to find both sides of the limit
thinkable (i.e., we should have to be able to think what cannot be
thought)."

"It will therefore only be in language that the limit can be set, and
what lies on the other side of the limit will simply be nonsense."

Now what is interesting about these passages for us is not the ingenious way in which they propose to escape from the dilemma which,
according to some critics, attaches to Kant's position,[25] but rather that
they indicate the interesting countinuity in his approach – an approach
characteristic of all his works, early and late. No, he says, as he is about
to lapse into Kantian language," – not to thought, but to the *expression*
of thoughts ..." The trick is to be performed at the level of language,
for it is there that our troubles arise and where therefore they can be
best managed.

But although translating these problems into linguistic terms, which
is Wittgenstein's distinctive achievement here, does of course make a
profound difference in our understanding of them and introduces new
possibilities and new ways of dealing with them, it would be a mistake, I
think, to say that Kant was himself completely unaware of them. "To
search in our daily cognition," he states, for example, in a passage in the
Prolegomena which indicates that he was not entirely blind to these
interesting possibilities, "for the concepts, which do not rest upon
particular experience, and yet occur in all cognition of experience, where
they as it were constitute the mere form of connexion, presupposes
neither greater reflexion nor deeper insight," he says there, "than to
detect in a language the rules of the actual use of words generally, and
thus to collect elements for a grammar. In fact both researches are very
nearly related."[26] This is, of course, an isolated passage. However, in
view of the way the central problem of the *Critique* is posed – viz., How
are synthetic a priori propositions possible? – it is not, after all,

---

[25] See, for example, Ayer's *Language, Truth and Logic* (New York: Dover Publications,
Inc., 1946), pp. 34–5.
[26] Edited in English by Dr. Paul Carus (La Salle: The Open Court Publishing Co., 1955),
p. 85. This passage in Kant has not gone unnoticed by analysts. It is used by Antony Flew
as a motto in his *Essays in Conceptual Analysis* (New York: Macmillan & Co., 1956).

considering this emphasis on logical structure and language, an un-characteristic one.

Kant did not, of course, carry out to any great extent this kind of reduction that is inherent in his very procedure, nor did he ever bother to explore the possibilities which he so interestingly raises in the passage from the *Prolegomena*. But Wittgenstein did. He saw these other possi-bilities and in working them out in the kind of detail he did, he gave that system of thought an entirely different direction and a new lease on life.

6

Let me conclude this chapter not with a summary but rather with two brief quotations from Mr. Drury's contribution to a Symposium on Wittgenstein.[27]

I find people writing and talking as if Wittgenstein knew little and cared less about the history of philosophy: as if he regarded his own work as abrogating all that had gone before him, and he confined all previous metaphysics to the limbo of the meaningless. This is a misunderstanding. In one of the earliest conversations I had with him he said: "Don't think I despise metaphysics or ridicule it. On the contrary, I regard the great metaphysical writings of the past as among the noblest productions of the human mind."

And finally:

We were discussing a suitable title for the book which later he called *Philosophical Investigations*. I foolishly suggested he should just call it "Philosophy." He was indignant. "How could I take a word like that which has meant so much in the history of mankind; as if my writings were anything more than a small fragment of philosophy?" I do not think Wittgenstein would ever have spoken of his work as a "revolution in philosophy." It was a way of thinking for which he knew he had a special talent and which threw light on all the traditional problems of philosophy.

---

[27] Reprinted in K. T. Fann's collection. See p. 68.

CHAPTER FOUR

SCHOPENHAUER

I

Of all the recent writers who have noted Schopenhauer's influence upon Wittgenstein, none have been more explicit than Miss Anscombe. "It is very much a popular notion of Wittgenstein," Miss Anscombe points out, "that he was a latter-day Hume; but any connections between them are indirect, and he never read more than a few pages of Hume."

If we look for Wittgenstein's philosophical ancestry, we should rather look to Schopenhauer; specifically, his "solipsism," his conception of "the limit" and his ideas on value will be better understood in the light of Schopenhauer than of any other philosopher. It is one of the oddities of the present day that Schopenhauer is often vaguely associated with Nietzsche and even with Nazism, and is thought to be some kind of immoralist, worshipper of power and praiser of suicide; it is not the mythical Schopenhauer of popular repute, but the actual Schopenhauer, that we should remember in connection with Wittgenstein.[1]

Miss Anscombe also explicitly informs us that it was "as a boy of sixteen" that "Wittgenstein had read Schopenhauer and had been greatly impressed by Schopenhauer's theory of the 'world as idea' (though not of 'the world as will')." "Schopenhauer then struck him," she says, "as fundamentally right, if only a few adjustments and clarifications were made."[2]

Miss Anscombe does not state whether Wittgenstein ever again returned to his study of Schopenhauer. If he did not, the impact of that first and last reading must indeed have been considerable, for not only Miss Anscombe but other Wittgenstein scholars as well have been struck by the Schopenhauerian tone of many of the passages of the *Notebooks* and *Tractatus* – works written some eleven to thirteen years after that first and (presumably) last reading.

[1] *An Introduction to Wittgenstein's Tractatus* (London: Hutchinson University Library, 1959), p. 12.
[2] *Ibid.*, pp. 11-12.

"We should remember," Miss Anscombe herself reminds us towards the conclusion of her study, "that Wittgenstein had been much impressed by Schopenhauer as a boy; many traces of this sympathy are to be found in the *Tractatus*."[3] "The notes show," Professor von Wright remarks in his biographical sketch of Wittgenstein, "how strong were the impressions that Wittgenstein had received from Schopenhauer."[4] "We can also see," Mr. Favrholdt writes, "that he has read attentively *Die Welt als Wille und Vorstellung*." "The passages on solipsism, will, and ethics in the *Tractatus*," he points out, "are conceived by Wittgenstein with Schopenhauer in mind."[5] And so on.

Although these scholars do not say that Wittgenstein did not again consult Schopenhauer, their remarks seem to imply that he did not. Assuming this to be so, it is difficult to see how they reconcile Wittgenstein's single reading of Schopenhauer at the age of sixteen with their explicit remarks regarding the extent of Schopenhauer's influence upon his work some thirteen years later. In addition, if it is indeed true, as Professor von Wright and the others attest, that Schopenhauer was one of the very few philosophers whose writings Wittgenstein admired,[6] then it seems difficult to believe that Wittgenstein never again returned to him after having read or studied him at this single period in his life. But there are other problems as well.

"If I remember rightly," Professor von Wright informs us, "Wittgenstein told me that he had read Schopenhauer's *Die Welt als Wille und Vorstellung* in his youth and that his first philosophy was a Schopenhauerian epistemological idealism. Of how this interest was related to his interest in logic and the philosophy of mathematics I know nothing, except that I remember his saying that it was Frege's conceptual realism which made him abandon his earlier idealistic views."[7]

[3] *Ibid.*, p. 168.
[4] *The Philosophical Review*, 64 (1955). A revised version of it forms the opening chapter to Norman Malcolm's beautiful and moving *Memoir of Wittgenstein* (London: Oxford University Press, 1958). See p. 9 of this work.
[5] *An Interpretation and Critique of Wittgenstein's Tractatus* (New York: Humanities Press, 1966), p. 220.
[6] What may even prove to be of greater interest and surprise is Professor von Wright's disclosure that "Wittgenstein held the writings of Otto Weininger in high regard" (p. 21). This is perhaps more remarkable, for however difficult it may be to reconcile ourselves to the fact that Wittgenstein was attracted to Schopenhauer, it requires a considerably more complicated adjustment to do so in the case of Weininger. Otto Weininger was born in Vienna on April 3, 1880 and died (by his own hand) on October 4, 1903 – at the age of 23. A year previously he published what turned out to be a sensational book, entitled *Sex and Character*. (See David Abrahamsen's study of Weininger, *The Mind and Death of a Genius*, New York: Columbia University Press, 1946). Future biographers of Wittgenstein will probably want to learn more than we presently know concerning Wittgenstein's interest in Weininger, whom he may even have known personally.
[7] *Ibid.*, p. 5.

Here, then, is one problem. For not only is it difficult to reconcile Wittgenstein's early and single reading of Schopenhauer (assuming this to be so) with the extent of its impact some thirteen years later, but it is also difficult to reconcile Wittgenstein's interests in logic, etc. with those he found in Schopenhauer (assuming these to be merely what have so far been acknowledged). The question therefore suggests itself whether perhaps we have not been mistaken about both these assumptions. Did Wittgenstein's interest in Schopenhauer continue, perhaps, beyond his youth, and did he perhaps see in Schopenhauer things which we and Professor von Wright have so far failed to appreciate?

In what follows I should like to argue that this must indeed have been so. To put it briefly, what I should here like to show is that among the things which caught Wittgenstein's fancy in Schopenhauer were a number which (whether he read them at the age of sixteen, or, as I am inclined to believe, later on) were not at all in conflict with his basic orientation. These have to do not only with ethics or aesthetics (which were to leave their traces on the *Tractatus*) but with logic and language (which were to leave their mark on his later thought).

Now to say this may seem strange, for Schopenhauer is certainly not generally known to have made any startling contributions to logic and language. But Miss Anscombe is correct: in pursuing this question it is not the mythical and popular but the actual Schopenhauer that we need keep in mind. And the actual Schopenhauer claimed to have made striking discoveries in just these areas – discoveries, as I should like to show here, which have their remarkable parallels in Wittgenstein's later works.[8]

---

[8] In proceeding to trace this influence it would perhaps be best to acknowledge that regardless of its nature and extent, it is not my intention to claim more knowledge concerning its precise direction and operation than I really possess. It would be difficult to substantiate any such claim. On the other hand, it would be a mistake to think that this influence, whatever its precise nature or direction, was of a general and diffuse sort. The fact is that it is not merely a matter of being able to point up in Schopenhauer Wittgenstein's interest in, say, language, for occasionally it is as specific and determinate as the direct borrowing of a key term – "family resemblance" (*Familienähnlichkeiten*), for example, which plays such a significant role in Wittgenstein's philosophy and which he took directly, I believe, from Schopenhauer who uses the term (and in a sense not unlike that later given to it by Wittgenstein) a number of times in his work. See, for example, *Die Welt als Wille und Vorstellung* (edited by Julius Frauenstädt, Leipzig, 1922), Vol. 2, p. 115; p. 183; and Vol. 3, p. 435. Both Haldane and Kemp (whose translation of the *World as Will and Idea* – London: Routledge & Kegan Paul, 1833 – I am using here) and E. F. J. Payne (*The World as Will and Representation*, Indian Hills: The Falcon's Wing Press, 1958), use "family likeness" as their translation of the phrase. (See, for example, Haldane and Kemp's translation in Vol. I, p. 201). This is the English phrase which Wittgenstein himself uses in the *Blue and Brown Books*. (See, for example, p. 17.) Miss Anscombe translates the term by way of the now familiar phrase "family resemblance" (see, for example, *Philosophical Investigations*, I, 67.) It is possible, of course, that Wittgenstein used both English expressions.

2

I will begin with Schopenhauer's small treatise on "The Art of Controversy."[9]

This little book by Schopenhauer is somewhat of a problem. It is not that the often crude advice on how to win arguments which it contains seems strange coming from a philosopher, for, as T. Bailey Saunders has already pointed out, it is quite obvious that "a good deal of its content is of an ironical character."[10] The problem is rather why Schopenhauer thought he was doing here something that had not, as far as he had been able to discover, been done before.[11] And this *is* a problem for the book contains numerous references to Aristotle and seems to be merely a treatise on what we now call "Common Fallacies." Yet there is a good deal to Schopenhauer's claim.

"Logic" and "Dialectic," Schopenhauer begins by saying, have been regarded both by the ancients and moderns as synonymous. This however is a mistake since the two can be easily distinguished and are not the same. If he were at liberty to do so, he would distinguish and define them as follows: "Logic" he would define as "the science of the laws of thought," that is, the study of the laws of thought which "reason follows when it is left to itself and not hindered ... or ... misled"; "Dialectic" he would define, on the other hand, as "the art of disputation," that is, the art of "intercourse between two rational beings who,

---

[9] Translated by T. Bailey Saunders (London: George Allen & Unwin Ltd., 1896). This treatise was published only posthumously. A briefer version of it was made public by Schopenhauer in the *Parerga*, under the heading *Zur Logik und Dialektik*. He had meant to write a whole treatise on the subject and had been collecting material from a very early time, he relates in the published extract, but (as happened with Wittgenstein with the *Philosophical Investigations*) he found he could no longer do it. Mr. Gardiner, in his recent book on Schopenhauer (Baltimore: Penguin Books, 1963) missed, I believe, a rather wonderful opportunity of enlightening his readers regarding the full extent of Schopenhauer's impact on Wittgenstein. Not, of course, that Mr. Gardiner fails to discuss this matter. On the contrary, he mentions Wittgensteins' name a number of times in his book (although only in connexion with the *Tractatus* and not the later works), and his doing so is one of the things which Mr. Ayer, the Editor of the series in which Mr. Gardiner's book appears, singles out for special mention in his Editorial Foreword to the book. "In particular, admirers of Wittgenstein," Mr. Ayer writes, "may be surprised to discover the extent to which his thought was influenced by Schopenhauer's." My only quarrel with Mr. Gardiner is that he failed to make this surprise as striking as (I hope to show here) the matter admits.

[10] Introduction, p. vi.

[11] With the possible exception of a lost work by Theophrastus, as he points out in a footnote (*Essays from Parerga and Paralipomena*, translated by T. Bailey Saunders, London: George Allen & Unwin Ltd., 1951, p. 13). In the published extract he mentions several other works in which something of a similar nature had been done (but done badly) – one, ironically, entitled *Tractatus logicus singularis* ... (See Frauenstädt, Vol. 6, p. 28).

because they are rational, ought to think in common," but who (because of "the disturbances which pure thought suffers through the difference of individuality") as a matter of fact often do not.[12]

Dialectic is thus the means which "disputants adopt in order to make good against one another their own individual thought."[13] It can thus also be defined as the "art of proving oneself right" – "Whether one has any reason for being so or not"; or the art "of attaining the appearance of truth, regardless of its substance."[14] Seen as such, its aim is victory, not truth.

It is for this reason as well that Dialectic has sometimes been defined, he continues, as the "Logic of Appearance," but this definition "is a wrong one, as in that case it could only be used to repel false propositions. But even when a man has the right on his side, he needs Dialectic in order to defend and maintain it; he must know what the dishonest tricks are, in order to meet them; nay, he must often make use of them himself, so as to best the enemy with his own weapons."[15] Seen in this light, a study of Dialectic is useful in informing us not only how such victory is to be attained but how some arguments manage to give the appearance of being sound when they are not.

Still it would be a mistake to think that "Dialectic" has "objective truth in view." But it ought not for this reason to be despised. "This very dishonesty, this persistence in a proposition which seems false even to ourselves," he points out, "has something to be said for it."[16] For it is possible, after all, that we may without knowing it be in the right or that our opponent's case may only seem to be true. Since argument will bring this out, to persist here is therefore valuable. A consideration of such "tactics" is therefore an important undertaking.

Aristotle, however, although not unaware of the importance of this discipline, "does not define the object of Dialectic as exactly," Schopenhauer says, "as I have done it here; for while he allows that its principal object is disputation, he declares at the same time that it is also the discovery of truth. ... He is aware that the objective truth of a proposition must be distinguished and separated from the way in which it is pressed home, and approbation won for it, but he fails to draw a sufficiently sharp distinction between these two aspects of the matter,

[12] *Essays*, p. 6.
[13] *Ibid.*
[14] *Ibid.*, p. 7.
[15] *Ibid.*, p. 11. Kant has already made a similar sort of suggestion. See the *Critique of Pure Reason*, A 777–B 805.
[16] P. 8.

so as to reserve Dialectic for the latter alone."[17] Such a sharper distinction needs to be drawn if the science of Dialectic is to be of value to us.

If we will do this we will find that Dialectic need have as little to do with truth as fencing does regarding who is in the right. There as here, "trust and parry is the whole business. Dialectic is the art of intellectual fencing; and it is only when we so regard it that we can erect it into a branch of knowledge."[18]

In fact "the science of Dialectic, in one sense of the word, is mainly concerned to tabulate and analyse dishonest stratagems, in order that in a real debate they may be at once recognized and defeated."[19]

"I am not aware," he writes, "that anything has been done in this direction, although I have made inquiries far and wide. It is, therefore, an uncultivated soil." To cultivate it properly we must, he says finally, turn to our own experience: "we must observe how in the debates which often arise in our intercourse with our fellowmen this or that stratagem is employed by one side or the other. By finding out the common elements in tricks repeated in different forms, we shall be enabled to exhibit certain general stratagems which may be advantageous, as well for our own use, as for frustrating others if they use them."

"What follows," he adds as a final comment, "is to be regarded as a first attempt."[20]

Now it is what follows that is so very puzzling. For what Schopenhauer proceeds to do, at great length, is to define and give examples of a large number of Common Fallacies: Figure of Speech, Irrelevant Conclusion, *Non Sequitur*, *Ad Populum*, Begging the Question, and so on. The discussion, in other words, seems very disappointing, illustrating, as it seems to do, Dialectic in that "one sense of the word" just mentioned – namely, learning how to identify and meet the dishonest tricks used in debates by one's opponents. Even, therefore, "as a first attempt," his analysis of stratagems, as he calls them, comes as something of a disappointment to us, covering ground which had already been well gone over by Aristotle, who is quoted and referred to extensively throughout the discussion.

Now although this is generally so, something does come out in the series of analyses which does fail to catch our attention and which connects in an interesting way with work done in the *World as Will and*

17 P. 10.
18 P. 12.
19 Pp. 12–13.
20 P. 13.

Idea – work which, as we shall see in a moment, is no longer such a far cry from that so familiar to us from the pages of Wittgenstein.

For although stratagems, Schopenhauer here goes on to explain, are simply "tricks" or "expedients" which come naturally to us in disputes, they are not always of the simple sort sometimes implied by those who have made a study of them, nor are they merely shady tricks of reasoning which deceive us, for just as we possess a *"natural Logic"* so we also possess a *"natural Dialectic"* with all that this implies. On the contrary, such simple sophisms as have been studied are obvious and "will deceive no one." There are some, however, which, because of their "subtle form" *are* "apt to mislead." And this is especially so "where the conceptions which are covered by the same word are related, and inclined to be interchangeable."

"It is never subtle enough to deceive," however, "if it is used intentionally; and therefore cases of it must be collected from actual and individual experience."[21] And this is what he now proceeds to do. The example of a systematically misleading expression which he chooses here, although somewhat lengthy, illustrates his method well and is sufficiently interesting to be quoted in its entirety.

I condemned the principle involved in the word *honour* as a foolish one; for, according to it, a man loses his honour by receiving an insult, which he cannot wipe out unless he replies with a still greater insult, or by shedding his adversary's blood or his own. I contended that a man's true honour cannot be outraged by what he suffers, but only and alone by what he does; for there is no saying what may befall any one of us. My opponent immediately attacked the reason I had given, and triumphantly proved to me that when a tradesman was falsely accused of misrepresentation, dishonesty, or neglect in his business, it was an attack upon his honour, which in this case was outraged solely by what he suffered, and that he could only retrieve it by punishing his aggressor and making him retract. Here, by a homonymy, he was foisting *civic honour*, which is otherwise called *good name*, and which may be outraged by libel and slander, on to the conception of *knightly honour*, also called *point d'honneur*, which may be outraged by insult. And since an attack on the former cannot be disregarded, but must be repelled by public disproof, so, with the same justification, an attack on the latter must not be disregarded either, but it must be defeated by still greater insult and a duel. Here we have a confusion of two essentially different things through the homonymy in the word *honour*, and a consequent alteration of the point in dispute.[22]

Although there is certainly a quite modern ring about his analysis here, which invites comment and comparison, it is still rather the other point

---

[21] *Essays*, p. 17.

[22] Pp. 17–18. Compare here Wittgenstein's remark from the *Philosophical Investigations* (I, 11): "What confuses us is the uniform appearance of words when we hear them spoken or meet them in scripts and print. For their *application* is not presented to us so clearly."

(what it was, precisely, that Schopenhauer thought he was doing for the first time) which I wish at the moment to explicate here. And that point is reaffirmed again in the very next "stratagem" where he states of Aristotle's example of it that it is "an obvious sophism, which will deceive no one." "Let us contrast it," instead, he says again, "with one drawn from actual experience."[23] And the example he gives is again one which illustrates the point he particularly wishes to make here, namely, that "stratagems" are not necessarily artificial devices which one may occasionally incorporate into one's speech for purposes of gaining victory; but rather that often they are the sorts of things which arise out of language itself and into which we innocently "blunder." These tend to assume forms which *are* extremely deceptive.

Now it is here where, I believe, he regarded himself, and, I think, with justice, as having made a new and major discovery. His handling of it in this little treatise is, however, brief and, in comparison with Wittgenstein, disappointing.[24] But he has a good deal more to say on the subject in his major work, the *World as Will and Idea*. There, as we will see in a moment, he tends to do more justice to himself, no longer confining his discussion to "sophisms" and the way they deceive, but to *language* and the way it *generally* tends to deceive. But even in the treatise it is still apparent, I think, that his discovery is not so much a matter of having noted something peculiar about common fallacies but rather of having noted something peculiar about language itself.

"Under Dialectic," Schopenhauer tells us in the *World as Will and Idea*, he understands:

in agreement with Aristotle ... the art of conversation directed to the mutual investigation of truth, especially philosophical truth. But a conversation of this kind necessarily passes more or less into controversy; therefore dialectic may also be explained as the art of disputation. We have examples and patterns of dialectic in the Platonic dialogues; but for the special theory of it, thus for the technical rules of disputation, eristics, very little has hitherto been accomplished.[25]

Now while Logic can have little practical use, Dialectic can be extremely useful, for where Dialectic is concerned we can sometimes with its

---

[23] P. 18.

[24] *Ibid.* It would be misleading to suggest that the whole of this brief treatise was written by him to be read along the lines argued here. There is much in it, for example, in which he merely seems to be covering old ground or engaging in banter (certain "tricks," he tells us, require "a good voice," or an "extreme degree of impudence," etc.) On the other hand, however, there is also much in it in which he is obviously exploring new territory, showing how the mind often quite innocently falls prey to puzzles and confusions which are linguistically generated.

[25] *The World* II, 285.

help take "the more or less intentionally deceptive argument of our opponent, which he advances under the garb and cover of continuous speech," and convict it "of logical errors."[26]

It will not perhaps surprise us to find that here again the kind of error which he seems to have in mind are none other than the traditional Aristotelian ones: "simple conversion of universal affirmative judgments, syllogisms with four terms, inferences from consequent to the reason, syllogisms in the second figure with merely affirmative premises, and many such."[27] But again, interestingly enough, he goes on to point out here that logical deduction is often exposed to deceptions which not only lack distinct names but are a good deal more intractable than those already so identified. And it is here that he now goes on to explore some new ground, as he himself so regards it.

It occurs in the course of his discussion of the history of the attempt to use diagrams (squares, lines, circles) to represent the relations between concepts. "Upon what this complete analogy between the relations of concepts, and those of figures in space, ultimately rests," he says, "I am unable to say." It was, however, "an exceedingly happy idea" and "a very fortunate circumstance for logic."[28] It is by means of such figures (spheres being his favourite here) that he now sets about to show how some concepts, because of their uncertain boundaries and vagueness, give rise to all sorts of bad philosophy and argument.

Correct and accurate conclusions may be arrived at if we carefully observe the relation of the spheres of concepts, and only conclude that one sphere is contained in a third sphere, when we have clearly seen that this first sphere is contained in a second, which in its turn is contained in the third. On the other hand, the art of sophistry lies in casting only a superficial glance at the relations of the spheres of the concepts, and then manipulating these relations to suit our purposes.[29]

"I am not aware that hitherto," he repeats here what we have already had occasion to hear him say earlier (revealing now however the true depth of his insight here) that "any one has traced the nature of all sophistry and persuasion back to this last possible ground of its existence, and referred it to the peculiar character of concepts, *i.e.*, to the procedure of reason itself."[30]

This is, I believe, an enormously interesting and revealing statement.

[26] II, 286.
[27] *Ibid.*
[28] I, 55.
[29] I, 63.
[30] I, 63–4.

At least two very important things are involved in it: one, his view that the real source of "sophistry" is to be located in processes natural to our reason (to our "*natural Dialectic*" as he put it elsewhere); and, two, that its vehicle is "concepts" – not this or that troublesome concept, but concepts as such. There are now, perhaps, more provocative and elaborate ways of stating these insights and those familiar with the work of Wittgenstein will know the words which he used to do that. That we are dealing here, however, with essentially similar views there can be little doubt. His further discussion here makes this even clearer.

To illustrate his point, Schopenhauer draws here a diagram consisting of a series of intersecting circles and shows how if one begins with a broad enough concept (he takes the example of ' travelling" – its pros and cons) it is possible for anyone by gradual stages (since the concepts "overlap") to "prove" almost anything one wishes. One should not, he says, attach too much importance to the example given (even though he sets aside an entire page to diagram it) for it is, as he admits, a trivial one; but what is important to see here is, he says, that "most scientific arguments, and especially philosophical demonstrations, are at bottom not much more than this."

In his essay on the "History of the Doctrine of the Ideal and Real," he goes on to give such an example. The essay is a sketch of the history of the attempt to solve the mind-body problem and the absurdities to which, he thought, some of these attempts (often "resting on the misuse of words," as he puts it) led their proponents. He ends his account with a few words on Hegel, who, according to him, derived his doctrine from Schelling, who in turn got it from Spinoza. "Schelling had, according to Spinoza's procedure, entitled the world "God." Hegel took this in its literal sense. Now since this word properly signifies a personal being, embracing, together with other qualities altogether incompatible with the word, that of omniscience, this was also transferred by him to the world," and with obvious absurd results.[31] It was with such "tricks," he adds finally, that Hegel held "the learned world of Germany for thirty years."[32]

---

[31] *Selected Essays of Schopenhauer*. Trans. by Ernest Belfort Bax (London: G. Bell & Sons, Ltd., 1914, p. 32).

[32] The note on which the essay ends is also not irrelevant. "You may also puzzle and bewilder your opponent," he says there, "by mere bombast; and the trick is possible, because a man generally supposes that there must be some meaning in words." "It is a well-known fact," he then leaves off by saying. "that in recent times some philosophers have practised this trick on the whole of the public with the most brilliant success." If these remarks tend to remind the reader of what some analysts have in our own day been saying about their colleagues, it should not come as a surprise, for that too, of course, was a favourite theme with

To return, however, to the *World as Will and Idea*. Every deduction from concepts is, he explains, "exposed" to such "deceptions," for the simple reason

that so many spheres lie partly within each other, and that their content is often vague and uncertain. This is illustrated by a multitude of demonstrations of false doctrines and sophisms of every kind. Syllogisms are indeed perfectly certain as regards form, but they are very uncertain on account of their matter, the concepts. For, on the one hand, the spheres of these are not sufficiently sharply defined, and, on the other hand, they intersect each other in so many ways that one sphere is in part contained in many others, and we may pass at will from it to one or another of these, and from this sphere again to others.[33]

And that is, I believe, substantially the view and diagnosis given later by Wittgenstein regarding the way in which words because of their vague and uncertain boundaries tend to lead us astray. In his *Remarks on the Foundations of Mathematics*, for example, Wittgenstein put it in this strikingly similar way, using here, as does Schopenhauer, the language of concepts: "We certainly see bits of the concepts, but we don't clearly see the declivities by which one passes into others."[34]

This account of the way concepts deceive is meant to be read (and Schopenhauer instructs us to do so) in the light of what he says in his "Art of Controversy." By supporting each other in the way they do, they seem to constitute a unified theory regarding the way in which our minds are deceived and held captive by language which both in outline and execution is remarkably similar to what can be found on the same theme in the later writings of Wittgenstein.

There are, of course, differences. How completely aware, for one thing, Schopenhauer was of the significance of his own discoveries here is difficult to say. That he thought he was doing something new is clear from his own explicit remarks on this matter. On the other hand, however, he very often tends to treat these things as really too absurd to be taken seriously, and this is especially the case whenever he comes to

---

Schopenhauer, as everyone who has come in contact with his work knows. And the connexion is even closer than that, as his comment on "pantheism" (in a short paper by that name), and on Schelling's definition of freedom – to choose two brief examples – plainly indicate. His "chief objection" to pantheism is, "that it says nothing" (*Essays*, p. 40). As to Schelling's definition of freedom, it is a definition, he says of it (in his own "Essay on the Freedom of the Will," trans. by Konstantin Kolenda, New York: The Liberal Arts Press, 1960, p. 85) which "may be of some use" for the catechism, "but in philosophy nothing is said by it and, consequently nothing can be done with it."

[33] I, 80–90. Schopenhauer also uses this device in his essay "Über Sprache und Worte" (p. 601). Compare here Wittgenstein's remark that "misunderstandings concerning the use of words" are "caused, among other things, by certain analogies between the forms of expression in different regions of language ..." (*Philosophical Investigations* I, 90).

[34] (Oxford: Basil Blackwell, 1956), p. 157.

discuss Hegel who, he believed, had perpetrated a kind of hoax on the German reading public and did not simply "blunder" into these errors. Wittgenstein, as we know, was to regard these matters in a different spirit and much more seriously. More consistently than Schopenhauer, he was to see in these curious mental processes "one of the most fertile sources of philosophic puzzlement,"[35] and the "nonsense" in which they often issued, an important nonsense. They were not regarded by him as "tricks."[36] It is certainly one of the ironies of recent philosophic history that many of his disciples should again so regard them.

To summarize: We have observed thus far how according to both philosophers, *conceptual confusion is something we are almost unavoidably led into; that this is so because of something either in our own nature or because our concepts, being ambiguous and lacking clear boundaries, give rise to superficial resemblances; that these resemblances have far-reaching consequences not only for ordinary discourse but for both science and philosophy.* But although this account of the way our language plays havoc with our thoughts is certainly strikingly similar to what can be found on this subject in Wittgenstein, it still leaves a number of rather important questions unanswered. What, more precisely, for example, is it either about ourselves or language that makes us so prone to be thus deceived? And what, if anything, furthermore, can we do to guard ourselves against these dangers and deceptions?

Schopenhauer is not silent on these questions. What he has to say about them, and others like them, have again their parallels in Wittgenstein, as we will see in a moment.

3

In turning to Schopenhauer's philosophy of language we leave behind what we might call Schopenhauer's and Wittgenstein's Special Theory of Linguistic Deception and turn to their General Theory.

---

[35] *The Blue and Brown Books*, p. 108.

[36] The closest he ever comes to using this sort of language is, as far as I can recall at the moment, in *Philosophical Investigations* (I, 290) where he remarks: "Perhaps this word 'describe' tricks us here ('*hat uns da vielleicht zum Besten*'). I say 'I describe my state of mind' and 'I describe my room.' You need to call to mind the differences between the language games." Since writing this there has appeared a publication consisting of students' notes of Wittgenstein's *Lectures and Conversations on Aesthetics, Psychology and Religious Belief* (edited by Cyril Barrett, Berkeley and Los Angeles: University of California Press, 1966) in which this word does appear. On p. 1 of this little book Wittgenstein is reported as saying: "We get into a new group of confusions; language plays us entirely new tricks."

Like so many other philosophers who have written on language, Schopenhauer's discussion of it issues from his attempt to come to grips not directly with it but rather with the general problem of the nature of concepts. It should not surprise us therefore if his various remarks on language lack that consistency which one might otherwise expect. On the other hand he has obviously read widely on the subject and thought deeply about it.

His earliest remarks are to be found in the *Fourfold Root of the Principle of Sufficient Reason.*[37] The only essential difference between the human race and animals, he states there, is man's ability to make abstractions.[38] These are formed, he goes on to explain, by dropping "something different belonging to each" and retaining only "what is the same in all." The result is a *"genus* of that species," "something general, and as such, not perceptible."[39] It is, as he explains it later in his major work the *World as Will and Idea,* "a throwing off of useless baggage for the sake of more easily handling the knowledge which is to be compared." We allow what is "unessential, and therefore only confusing, to fall away from the real things, and work with few but essential determinations thought in the abstract."[40]

These abstractions or representations, thus sublimated and therefore no longer perceptible, would entirely vanish from our consciousness were they not fixed and retained in our minds by arbitrary signs. These signs are words.[41]

But although this reduction of the knowledge of the perceptible world to abstract conceptions "is the fundamental business of the Reason, and can only take place by means of language," the two – thought and language – should not be confused, for they are not identical.[42]

Conceptions are certainly not to be identified or "confused with pictures of the imagination, these latter being intuitive and complete, therefore individual representations." For even when used to represent a conception, such a picture or "phantasm" ought to be distinguished from a conception, for such pictures are never adequate representations of their objects or conceptions, and some conceptions (triangle in general or dog in general, for example) are simply incapable of being so

---

[37] (London: George Bell & Sons, 1889).
[38] P. 114.
[39] P. 116.
[40] *The World* II, 235.
[41] *Fourfold*, p. 116.
[42] P. 117.

pictured.[43] In view of this, Aristotle obviously went too far "in thinking that no reflection is possible without pictures of the imagination."[44] Hume and Rousseau (but not Kant) understood these matters better.

Schopenhauer might have mentioned Berkeley's name as well, for there is obviously a great deal of Berkeley in his discussion here. There is also, however, as the following quotations show, a great deal which bears a strong resemblance, at least in tone, to what can be found in Wittgenstein.

Speech, as an object of outer experience, is obviously nothing more than a very complete telegraph, which communicates arbitrary signs with the greatest rapidity and the finest distinctions of difference. But what do these signs mean? How are they interpreted? When some one speaks, do we at once translate words into pictures of the fancy, which instantaneously flash upon us, arrange and link themselves together, and assume form and colour according to the words that are poured forth, and their grammatical inflections? What a tumult there would be in our brains while we listened to a speech, or to the reading of a book? But what actually happens is not this at all. The meaning of a speech is, as a rule, immediately grasped, accurately and distinctly taken in, without the imagination being brought into play.[45]

Supposing I teach someone the use of the work "yellow" by repeatedly pointing to a yellow patch and pronouncing the word. On another occasion I make him apply what he has learnt by giving him the order, "choose a yellow ball out of this bag." What was it that happened when he obeyed my order? I say "possibly just this: he heard my words and took a yellow ball from the bag." Now you may be inclined to think that this couldn't possibly have been all; and the kind of thing that you would suggest is that he imagined something yellow when he *understood* the order, and then chose a ball according to his image. To see that this is not *necessary* remember that I could have given him the order, "Imagine a yellow patch." Would you still be inclined to assume that he first imagines a yellow patch to match the first? (Now I don't say that this is not possible. Only, putting it in this way immediately shows you that it need not happen.)[46],

It would seem, therefore, according to Schopenhauer, that since thought or conception is not to be confused with images, it must be identified with words. For, according to him, all thinking "necessitates either words or pictures of the imagination: without one or other of these it has nothing to hold by."[47]

But Schopenhauer seems to waver on this point, as indeed Wittgen-

[43] P. 120.
[44] P. 122.
[45] *The World* I, 51.
[46] *Blue Book*, pp. 11–12.
[47] *Fourfold*, p. 121.

stein does too.[48] In the *World as Will and Idea* the former speaks of "words representing ... ideas"[49] and goes on to say explicitly: "Such an important tool of the intellect as the *concept* evidently cannot be identical with the *word*, this mere sound, which as an impression of sense passes with the moment, or as a phantasm of hearing dies away with time."[50] In view of what he has just said, however, that seems like a contradiction.

It would not, I think, be correct to try to resolve this contradiction by saying that what he means is that although *logically* it is always possible (perhaps even necessary) to distinguish between the conception and the word which fixes it firmly in our minds, *psychologically* it is not possible to carry on thinking without the aid of words. For in the *World as Will and Idea*[51] he allows that occasionally words are a burden to the process of thought, a process which can be carried on more rapidly without them.[52] But, of course, if thinking can be carried on without words, what kind of process is it and how is it carried out? But these are questions which no one who has tried to maintain the separation of language from thought has yet been able to answer.

But this separation of thought from language (however this is to be justified or explained) enables Schopenhauer to make some interesting points about language, points that seem familiar to readers of Wittgenstein. "Words and speech are thus," he remarks:

the indispensable means of distinct thought. But as every means, every machine, at once burdens and hinders, so also does language; for it forces the fluid and modifiable thoughts, with their infinitely fine distinctions of difference, into certain rigid, permanent forms, and thus in fixing also fetters them. This hindrance is to some extent got rid of by learning several languages. For in these the thought is poured from one mould into another, and somewhat alters its form in each, so that it becomes more and more freed from all form and clothing, and thus its own proper nature comes more distinctly into consciousness, and it recovers again its original capacity for modification.[53]

But not only words or language have such a cramping effect on the mind – ideas and theories also take their toll. Speaking about certain scientific theory which have had this unfortunate effect he declares that it is far better in all such instances to confess our ignorance "than to bar

---

[48] Compare, for example, *Notebooks*, p. 82 and *Blue Book*, p. 41 with what he says in the *Philosophical Investigations* I, 32.

[49] *The World* I, 51.

[50] II, 234-5.

[51] II, 238.

[52] See also *Fourfold*, p. 118.

[53] *The World* II, 238-9.

the way of future knowledge by bad theories"[54] – a remark which should be compared with what Wittgenstein says in his *Philosophical Investigations*, namely, "An unsuitable type of expression is a sure means of remaining in a state of confusion. It as it were bars the way out."[55]

Because of the nature of their formation, abstractions carry with them, Schopenhauer argues further, certain very grave dangers. "The true kernel of all knowledge is that reflection which works with the help of intuitive representations; for it goes back to the fountain-head, to the basis of all conceptions."[56] Abstractions, formed as they are, as we have seen, by a kind of process of rarefaction, stand tó such primary sources of knowledge as "the upper stories of the building of reflection" to "the ground floor."[57] Rational talk which is composed of combinations of such abstract conceptions may therefore "render the result of given conceptions clearer." It does not, however, "strictly speaking, bring anything new to light."[58]

Philosophical systems which confine themselves to such very general conceptions, without going down to the real, are little more than mere juggling with words. For since all abstraction consists in thinking away, the further we push it the less we have left over. Therefore, if I read those modern philosophemes which move constantly in the widest abstractions, I am soon quite unable, in spite of all attention, to think almost anything more in connection with them; for I receive no material for thought, but am supposed to work with mere empty shells, which gives me a feeling like that which we experience when we try to throw very light bodies; the strength and also the exertion are there, but there is no object to receive them, so as to supply the other moment of motion. If any one wants to experience this let him read the writings of the disciples of Schelling, or still better of the Hegelians.[59]
(Cf. here the *Philosophical Investigations*: "We have got on to slippery ice where there is no friction and so in a certain sense the conditions are ideal, but also, just because of that, we are unable to walk. We want to walk: so we need friction. Back to the rough ground!")[60]

But what impels such people to engage in this empty verbiage? It is certainly not limited to the Hegelians. "A tendency of the mind to work

[54] III, 62.
[55] I, 339.
[56] *Fourfold*, p. 122.
[57] *The World* I, 53.
[58] *Fourfold*, p. 123.
[59] *The World* II, 235–6. Wittgenstein's remark quoted here also bears a striking similarity to Kant's Dove Analogy in the Introduction to the *Critique*. To think that because we seem to get on so well with concepts formed within the limits of experience (intuition) we might even get on better by freeing ourselves entirely from these limitations, is to be like "the light dove, who cleaving the air in her free flight, and feeling its resistance, might imagine that its flight would be still easier in empty space."
[60] I, 107.

with such abstract and too widely comprehended conceptions had shown itself almost at all times." "It may ultimately rest," he suggests here, "upon a certain indolence of the intellect, which finds it too difficult a task to be constantly controlling thought by perception."[61] (Cf. here Wittgenstein's *Blue Book*: "What makes it difficult for us to take this line of investigation is our craving for generality . . . the contemptuous attitude towards the particular case.")[62]

Often, however, it simply results from an abuse of words.

Locke has already shown at length that most disagreements in philosophy arise from a false use of words. For the sake of illustration just glance for a moment at the shameful misuse which philosophers destitute of thoughts make at the present day of the words substance, consciousness, truth, and many others.,[63]
No conception has been more misused in philosophy than that of *cause*, by means of the favourite trick or blunder of conceiving it too widely, taking it too generally, through abstract thinking. Since Scholasticism, indeed properly since Plato and Aristotle, philosophy has been for the most part a *systematic misuse of general conceptions*.[64]
But everywhere, as here, such unduly wide conceptions, under which, therefore, more was subsumed that their true content would have justified, there have arisen false principles, and from these false systems.,[65]

Philosophy, as a matter of fact, pursued this path "down to the time of Locke and Kant, who at last bethought themselves as to the origin of conceptions. Indeed we find Kant himself, in his earliest years, still upon the path." He might have avoided these pitfalls had "he gone back to the *source* of these conceptions and to their *true content* which is determined thereby. For then he would have found as the source and content of *substance* simply matter."[66] (Cf. here the *Philosophical Investigations*: "In such a difficulty always ask yourself: How did we *learn* the meaning of this word ("good" for instance)? From what sort of examples? In what language-games? Then it will be easier for you to see that the word must have a family of meanings.")[67]

Language, however, demands our respect. "Our ancestors did not make the words without attaching to them a definite meaning, in order, perhaps, that they might lie ready for philosophers who might possibly come centuries after and determine what ought to be thought in connection with them; but they denoted by them quite definite con-

[61] II, 211.
[62] Pp. 17–18.
[63] II, 141.
[64] II, 211.
[65] II, 212.
[66] II, 212.
[67] I, 77.

ceptions." Such common usage should be attended to and respected. If a certain explanation, for example, agrees "with the use of language at all times and among all peoples" then this is "a circumstance" which should "not be regarded as merely accidental or arbitrary," but should "be seen to arise from the distinction of which every man is conscious ... in accordance with which consciousness he speaks, though certainly he does not raise it to the distinctness of an abstract definition."[68]

On the contrary, "the agreement" on such points "between all languages ... proves that here we have to do with no mere figure of speech, but that the verbal expression is determined by a deeply-rooted feeling of the inner nature of things."[69] Lichtenberg was quite right: "... a good deal of wisdom" is "deposited in language."[70] "It is hardly likely that we have laid it all there ourselves, but rather that a great deal of wisdom really lies there."[71]

In their original context these no doubt remarkable thoughts with their close modern parallels tend perhaps to have a more limited and more specific application than I have given them here. In divesting them of their specific applications, however, I do not believe I have necessarily read more into them than they themselves really contain. For however we may wish to look at them, there can be little doubt, I think. that we have here in undeveloped form some of the key ideas of Wittgenstein's later philosophy. There is, of course, even here much that is still missing; but, on the other hand, such well-known theses as, for example, *the view that philosophic confusion has its source in language, that such confusions can be avoided or resolved by attending to particular usage, that although our craving for generality tends to work against our doing so, usage is and must be, nevertheless, the final arbiter,* cannot but remind us of their familiar counterparts in Wittgenstein's later philosophy.

---

[68] II, 140.
[69] *On the Will in Nature* (London: George Bell & Sons, 1889), p. 325.
[70] *Ibid.*, p. 322.
[71] *Ibid.* Schopenhauer's appeal to language and the confidence which he places in it will remind the reader of Austin's now notorious remark in "A Plea for Excuses": "... our common stock of words embodies all the distinctions men have found worth drawing, and the connexions they have found worth marking, in the lifetimes of many generations: these surely are likely to be more numerous, more sound, since they have stood up to the long test of the survival of the fittest, and more subtle, at least in all ordinary and reasonable practical matters, than any that you or I are likely to think up in our armchairs of an afternoon – the most favoured alternative method." (Reprinted in *Philosophical Papers*, Oxford: At the Clarendon Press, 1961), p. 130.

4

We have seen thus far some of the ways in which Schopenhauer seems to have anticipated several of the key points of Wittgenstein's Special Theory of Language, and also how he seems to have anticipated certain important points in his General Theory. It remains now to observe some further similarities between the two philosophers regarding their conception of the nature of philosophy itself.

Like his Special and General theories of Language, Wittgenstein's view of the nature of philosophy, positively viewed, is probably too well-known to require description here. Some of its essential points, however, are that it begins not just with wonder but with "puzzlement"; that its business is analysis; that it has a status different from that of the sciences; that it solves problems by dissolving them. Although Schopenhauer's philosophy is in numerous ways unlike Wittgenstein's (if indeed one may say that Wittgenstein *had* a philosophy), he seems, however, to have taken a remarkably similar view of philosophy, if one may judge by the quotations which follow.

"A man becomes a philosopher," Schopenhauer remarks in the *World as Will and Idea*, "by reason of a certain perplexity, from which he seeks to free himself."

"But what distinguishes the false philosopher from the true is this: the perplexity of the latter arises from the contemplation of the world itself, while that of the former results from some book, some system of philosophy which is before him."[72]

To be a philosopher, however, involves more than simply being receptive to "the forms of the visible world." For "one may have the greatest susceptibility for artistic beauty, and the soundest judgment in regard to it without being able to give an abstract and strictly philosophical justification of the nature of the beautiful." Or, again, "one may be very noble and virtuous, and may have a tender conscience, which decides with perfect accuracy in particular cases, without on that account being in a position to investigate and explain in the abstract the ethical significance of action."[73]

It is the ability to deal with abstractions that distinguishes the philosopher from the ordinary man. It is also only then that we truly experience the need for philosophy. For "as long as we continue to

[72] I, 41.
[73] I, 309–10.

perceive, all is clear, firm, and certain. There are neither questions nor doubts nor errors; we desire to go no further, can go no further, we find rest in perceiving, and satisfaction in the present. . . . But with abstract knowledge, with reason, doubt and error appear."[74]

Philosophy is the attempt to resolve these doubts and free ourselves of these errors. It may be defined as the "knowledge of the identical in different phenomena, and of difference in similar phenomena."[75] (Cf. here *Philosophical Investigations*: "The language-games are . . . *objects of comparison* which are meant to throw light on the facts of our language by way not only of similarities, but also of dissimilarities.")[76]

In this it differs completely from the sciences and is not on a level with them. For philosophy deals with its material from the highest and most universal point of view. As such it is of great service to them, for "empirical sciences pursued for their own sake and without philosophical tendency are like a face without eyes," and those occupied in the investigation of the individual sciences may be compared:

to those Geneva workmen of whom one makes only wheels, another only springs, and a third only chains. The philosopher, on the other hand, is like the watchmaker, who alone produces a whole out of all these which has motion and significance. They may also be compared to the musicians of an orchestra, each of whom is master of his own instrument; and the philosopher, on the other hand, to the conductor, who must know the nature and use of every instrument, yet without being able to play them all, or even one of them, with great perfection.[77]

(Cf. here the *Tractatus*: "Philosophy is not one of the natural sciences."[78] "Philosophy settles controversies about the limits of natural sciences.")[79]

In attempting to deal with its material in this way, however, philosophy has often gone astray and made false starts. The reason for this is that "the phenomena of the world which have to be explained present countless ends to us, of which one only can be the right one; they resemble an intricate tangle of thread, with many false end-threads hanging from it. He who finds the right one can disentangle the whole."[80]

---

[74] I, 45.
[75] I, 143.
[76] I, 130.
[77] II, 318–19.
[78] 4.111.
[79] 4.113.
[80] From "Fragments of the History of Philosophy," trans. by Belfort Bax and Bailey Saunders (*Philosophy of Arthur Schopenhauer*, New York: Tudor Publishing Co., 1936), p. 168. For a further use of this metaphor, which Wittgenstein was to use in a strikingly different way see also II, 439.

(Cf. here the *Notebooks*: "Just don't pull the knot tight before being certain that you have got hold of the right end.")[81]

What has prevented others from disentangling the thread properly is not, as some may perhaps think the false appearances of things or the weakness of the understanding. It is rather "the preconceived opinion, the prejudice which as a bastard *a priori*, opposes itself to the truth, and then resembles a contrary wind which drives the ship back from the direction in which the land lies, so that rudder and sail work in vain."[82] (Cf. here the *Philosophical Investigations*: "The confusions which occupy us arise when language is like an engine idling, not when it is doing work.")[83]

Once abolished, however, these preconceptions and "these problems would then be not, indeed, solved, but would have entirely vanished, and their expression would have no more meaning."[84] (Cf. here the *Philosophical Investigations*: "The clarity that we are aiming at is indeed *complete* clarity. But this simply means that the philosophical problems should completely disappear.")[85]

5

No one who knows the writings of Wittgenstein at all well can fail to be impressed with these remarkable similarities.[86] The reason, it seems to me, we have till now failed to note and appreciate them, especially where the later works are concerned, is because, like Professor von Wright, we have tended to believe that these later writings of Wittgenstein are completely without precedent, having, as he has put it, "no ancestors in philosophy."[87] But we need only heed Miss Anscombe's call that in considering these matters it is the actual Schopenhauer and

---

[81] P. 47. Cf. also *Zettel*, ed. by G. E. M. Anscombe and G. H. von Wright, trans. G. E. M. Anscombe (Oxford: Basil Blackwell, 1967), #452: "Philosophy unties knots in our thinking; hence its result must be simple, but philosophizing has to be as complicated as the knots it unties."

[82] "On Philosophy and Its Method," *ibid*, p. 248.

[83] I, 132.

[84] "Some Reflections on the Antithesis of the Thing-In-Itself and Phenomenon," *ibid*, p. 261.

[85] I, 133.

[86] It is interesting to remark in this connexion that Schopenhauer's major work, *The World as Will and Idea*, ends with a chapter on "Epiphilosophy" (what we would now call "meta-philosophy") in which he subjects philosophy itself to investigation. As such it is, like indeed the above, one of the early sustained discussions of a problem which has only in our day become an issue in philosophy.

[87] *Ibid.*, p. 15.

not the "mythical Schopenhauer of popular repute" that we must keep in mind in order to see that there is indeed much in the actual Schopenhauer that we have overlooked. To come to see this is to come to appreciate Wittgenstein's admiration for him and to recognize the true dimensions of the literary debt which he owed to him. Although this debt had to do with matters we rarely associate with Schopenhauer's name, they are, nevertheless, as I have tried to show here, an integral part of Schopenhauer's work.[88]

[88] In addition to our failure to recognize these new and striking ideas in Schopenhauer, what has perhaps prevented us from appreciating Wittgenstein's admiration for him is the nature and written quality of Schopenhauer's work. Although clear and elegant, it is a philosophy built almost entirely out of a seemingly endless series of analogies, similes and metaphors, many of them highly suspicious to one influenced by Wittgenstein. Such things (now seen to be pernicious and offensive) are precisely what, as many philosophers are now inclined to say, Wittgenstein's own philosophy was designed to fight and serve to deter. If Wittgenstein did indeed, therefore, read and admire the writings of Schopenhauer and was influenced by them, both the admiration and the influence must have been of a highly subtle and even perhaps a reactionary sort. I believe, however, that it would be a mistake to think that Wittgenstein responded to Schopenhauer only by reacting against him. Wittgenstein must have known that, like himself, Schopenhauer was intensely aware of the deceptions of language and of the pitfalls and dangers of mixing one's categories. On the contrary, Schopenhauer had even written a whole book on the subject, his doctoral dissertation, *The Fourfold Root of the Principle of Sufficient Reason.* His own use of metaphor, furthermore, as readers of his works well know, is frequently preceded by such qualifying and interesting expressions as "... if fond of similes ...," "... this somewhat too pictorial and absurd simile ...," "... if by metaphorical extension, we ...," etc. There are, however, of course, also such expressions, no less interesting, as "... it is almost more than a mere simile ...," "... this analogy may appear somewhat overdrawn, but ...," in which he makes it clear to his readers that in the matters under discussion we are indeed reaching "the limits of language." But that, he felt, should not prevent us from proceeding with our search. "Things which we cannot get at directly," he remarked in this connection, "we must make comprehensible to ourselves by means of an analogy." (*The World*, III, 99). "Certainly," he said in a similar context, "we fall here into mystical and figurative language," but it is the only language in which anything can be said on this entirely transcendent theme" (*The World*, III, 75). Statements such as these, whatever else they are indicative of, are surely not indicative of a man who has fallen victim to the deceptions of language. It does not therefore seem possible that Wittgenstein thought that Schopenhauer had been so deceived or "bewitched." It is, of course, possible that the idea that such dangers exist and that other people have indeed fallen victim to them, to say nothing of Schopenhauer's positive statements on these matters, did first suggest itself to him as a result of his reading of Schopenhauer.

CHAPTER FIVE

THE WILL TO METAPHYSICS: A BRIEF SUMMARY

I

For half a century or so now metaphysics has been subjected to a new kind of attack. New sorts of questions have been asked of it, and new objections raised against it. In particular, two things have tended to dominate this debate: one, that metaphysics is impossible, for the kind of knowledge it is after is in principle unattainable; and, secondly, that the will or desire to attain it is traceable to certain linguistic and psychological causes. The second of these claims has of course a ring about it that is distinctly more modern than the first, but neither of them is, as we have seen, really new. It was Kant, as I have tried to show here, who was the first to argue both of these theses: the first throughout the whole of the *Critique*, the second in the Transcendental Dialectic.

But although Kant was in this sense, perhaps, responsible for the course of recent speculation regarding metaphysics, and although he too might perhaps have been guilty – as some indeed have claimed he was – of taking a too narrow view of the logic of our mental operations, he at least did not make the mistake of thinking that there was some thing absurd about our attempt to attain such knowledge, or that it rested upon some simple and absurd error. Nor did, as we have also seen, Wittgenstein. For him, as for Kant, the pursuit of metaphysics was still a question of human frailty and not of human folly and, like Kant, he brought his whole thought to bear upon it.

But the greater majority of analysts have believed this. In what has preceded I have tried to explain how this has come about.

Partly this was due, as we have seen, to Wittgenstein's failure to resolve and work off the various tensions and contradictions in his thought, tensions and contradictions stemming from the diverse literary sources from which he gained his inspiration. The pressure of these influences upon him drew him in conflicting directions, leading him to believe that, on the one hand, philosophical puzzlement is a product of linguistic confusion (Schopenhauer), yet on the other hand that its source lies in needs deep in our nature (Kant); that what lies beyond the area amenable to skill is nonsense (Schopenhauer), yet that it is an important kind of nonsense (Kant), and so on.

If Wittgenstein did not resolve or work off these tensions, neither of course did his disciples. Breaking up into two separate camps, they merely carried each of these strands of his thought to their extremes and read into them what they ostensibly appeared to say. And this despite the fact that, like Kant, he plainly believed that the perplexity of reason is a *logical* and not a *pathological* condition, and that a linguistic confusion is never a simple or straightforward thing, it almost always being impossible to say just where it begins to mislead. Nor were all points about language, philosophically interesting. "I ought, perhaps, finally to repeat," Moore reports in this connexion, "what I said in the first part of this article namely, that he held that though the "new subject" must say a great deal about language, it was only necessary for it to deal with those points about language which have led, or are likely to lead, to definite philosophical puzzles or errors."[1] "I think he certainly thought," Moore goes on to say, "that some philosophers nowadays have been misled into dealing with linguistic points which have no such bearing, and the discussion of which therefore, in his view, forms no part of the proper business of a philosopher."[2]

That there is much in Wittgenstein, however, which can mislead in the way in which he apparently thought his disciples were misled is of course obvious to an outside observer. Wittgenstein could not have been unaware of this. What disturbed him, however, was something else, something which I think we can now fairly well reconstruct.

Long before they were to become aware of this, he began, I believe, to suspect that the tool he developed was really too crude for the sort of close work which others (following what they believed was his own example) were putting it to.[3] Yet, he also felt, the practice of analysis by others made it also appear a good deal more vulnerable than he thought it should be and seemed to bring into question points of doctrine which he instinctively felt were unshakable and universal.

With what has gone before it is not difficult to see why he should have

---

[1] "Wittgenstein's Lectures," p. 317.
[2] *Ibid.*
[3] The tendency more recently to speak of "models" and how they colour our thinking rather than of misleading analogies and metaphors is a recognition of this fact.

felt this way. He had, whether his disciples at present wish to admit it or not, quite obviously drunk deeply at the well of Kant. From Kant he had learned, as I tried to show above, the role which the *forms of judgment* play in the economy of our thought. As a result of his contact with Schopenhauer, however, (or, perhaps, even while pursuing his thoughts about Kant), he came to see that what Kant had taught applied to language itself. He had already undertaken this sort of reduction in the *Tractatus* and so he now systematically substituted *forms of expression* for Kant's forms of judgment – retaining, at the same time however, Kant's *transcendental* notion of Dialectic.

Earlier we explored the results of this new reduction or translation and pointed out the difficulty it tends to give rise to, and I will therefore not take the reader's time to restate it here. What, however, we can now perhaps see more clearly is Wittgenstein's reasons for feeling as apprehensive as he did regarding the ways in which his ideas were being applied and developed by his disciples. For although not himself unaffected by his contact with Schopenhauer and all that he had learned from him, it was nevertheless – so at least it seems to me when looked at in this way – the emerging Schopenhauerian emphasis in the works of his successors which began to puzzle and worry him. For that emphasis not only tended to take the force out of such notions (obviously so important to him) as "grammatical illusion," "craving for generality," "urge to misunderstand," "Depth grammar," etc. but also tended to throw in doubt the whole undertaking. By disengaging it, as they apparently did, from the transcendentalism of the dialectic they made the deception appear almost too perverse, too absurd.

They, of course, did not look at this in this way at all. Unaware that the Wittgensteinian system was a product of two diverse literary traditions between which it tried to maintain a delicate balance, they simply responded to those elements in it which they found congenial. The fact was, I believe, that Wittgenstein's work reminded them not of Kant, and not of Schopenhauer but (as Miss Anscombe has correctly noted) of Hume, and especially of his *Dialogues Concerning Natural Religion*.

The immense popularity of this little book, especially in recent decades, has never, it seems to me, been properly explained. Certainly it has not achieved this popularity because of its subject matter. On the contrary, this has rather tended to detract the attention of its readers from its peculiar qualities as a model of and exercise in philosophical analysis – of the sort, in fact, which even a quick reading of

Wittgenstein would seem to suggest that he recommended and even tried himself to practice. For here was a work with some very striking results based entirely on an extended exploration and analysis of a linguistic fallacy. Here was indeed a case where "a grammatical analogy" by being "worked out in detail" was exposed for what it was. Obviously this was something worthwhile emulating.

It took British philosophy some hundred years ,however, to recover from its fascination with the havoc that little work had created before it could examine dispassionately the method or methods which enabled it to carry out this remarkable piece of demolition. This was obviously not an easy task, for even at the end of that long period, and for many years after, there were still some who had not yet worked their way out of the debris. Pringle-Pattison and A. E. Taylor (among others), for example, were still as late as 1917 and 1921 trying to maintain that it was Cleanthes who won the debate in the *Dialogues*.

Those however who had worked their way out of the debris and had come under Wittgenstein's influence quickly realized that the logical tools which Hume had used in demolishing the Argument from Design were highly portable ones, easily adaptable – so at least they thought – to other problems and tasks. They were also quick to see the immense advantages that were to be gained from being able to discuss a problem whose solution or analysis neither disturbed nor involved any deep-seated prejudices or commitments either on the part of the investigator himself or others – whose solution, in fact, really left the basic issue as it found it. For after all Hume's discussion does not revolve around the question of God's *existence* – on the contrary, *that* seems to be taken for granted – but only around the question whether the Argument from Design which claims to prove He does exist, succeeds in doing so or not; whether, that is to say, it is a sound argument or not. And *that* question, of course, regardless how it is answered, leaves entirely unaffected (what is so difficult to discuss dispassionately) the question of His *being*. This kind of division of labor proved immensely attractive.

It proved to be also, however, the main source of difference between Wittgenstein's practice of analysis and theirs. For not only did this mislead them into dealing, as he put it, with linguistic points which no longer had any bearing on philosophy, but their almost exclusive reliance upon formal logical techniques widened this difference still further, leading them, unlike him, to adopt extreme and paradoxical positions.[4]

4 Note, for example, the way in which Wittgenstein handles the problem of thought and

Mainly, however, unlike him they could no longer say just why such analogies, equivocations, etc. should so inveterately mislead. That they did was for Wittgenstein guaranteed by the transcendentalism of the dialectic. They however, no longer had anything of the kind to fall back on. Having no other explanation available, they simply set it down to man's stupidity and folly. Little wonder that Wittgenstein came to regard their work as a "mangling" of this. Nor were those who tried to provide depth by searching the philosopher's unconscious any more faithful to his doctrines. Although his writings here too lent themselves to this kind of corruption, it was in its way as severe a falling off as the other.

2

It has sometimes been said that most of the great turning points in philosophy have taken place as a result of certain revisions in Logic or Method.[5] Among the great logical innovators, in this sense, the names of Aristotle, Hegel and Descartes come quickly to mind. To this list one could add, among others, the names of Locke, Hume and Kant. Each of these philosophers prided himself upon having discovered "a new method" – one which, they claimed, enabled them to solve, at long last, all the problems of philosophy: with Descartes it was, as we know, the "Sceptical Method," with Locke the "Historical, plain Method," with Hume the "Experimental Method," and with Kant the "Transcendental Method."

Wittgenstein belongs to this tradition, and in this sense he did in a way bring about a kind of "revolution in philosophy." For Wittgenstein discovered something about the logic of common fallacies which others should long ago have realized, namely, that although they were indeed common, they were sometimes far from simple – on the contrary, that some of them are capable of great subtlety and exercise an influence

language and the way in which it has been handled by those who have become aware of it as a result of their reading of Wittgenstein. Their almost total commitment to the merely logical aspects of the case leads them to results which Wittgenstein's own analysis, because of its enormously diversified nature generally manages to avoid. This is, I believe, typical. See the writer's paper "Thought and Language," *Dialogue*, Vol. 3, No. 2 (1964).

[5] Ryle makes a related remark in his book *Dilemmas*: "With a negligible number of exceptions," he says there, "every philosopher of genius and nearly every philosopher of even high talent from Aristotle to the present day has given himself some schooling in some parts of Formal Logic, and his subsequent philosophical reasonings have exhibited the effects upon him of this self-schooling, including sometimes his revolts against it." (p. 112).

upon our thinking that is more exacting and far-reaching than had ever been suspected before. How much of his own work, like the work of others[6] – almost the whole of Linguistic Analysis in fact – is a matter of the application to philosophical discussion of the test of common fallacy is evident everywhere in his writings.

It is, of course, true, as I have tried to show here, that these insights are already to be found elsewhere – especially in Schopenhauer and Kant. But he was the first to see their full value and to make such wide-spread use of them. He was also the first to try to combine and harmonize them. That he should have tried to do so by way of a therapeutic or clinical terminology should not (considering the time in which he wrote) be surprising to us.

The rest seemed almost inevitable. For having found such a vocabulary and being inclined to believe, like Kant and Schopenhauer before him, that philosophy is essentially an *activity*, it took only a small step to see that this activity was a matter, not of Dialectic as in Schopenhauer, nor of Transcendental Logic as in Kant, but of *dialogue* – a dialogue to be carried on with oneself with the object of getting rid of the "troubles in our thoughts" and of dispelling "puzzlement" and "confusion."

But however interesting and ingenious this new fusion of the clinical with the transcendental and dialectical proved to be, for the subsequent development of Analysis it was simply disastrous. For here too it was not long before some (and even Wittgenstein himself on occasion) began to say that the "troubles" are ones to which somehow only philosophers are susceptible and that to cure them not dialogue is required but simply "talk." That it should have been soon discovered that, in view of the circumstances, there is really nothing to talk about [7](or to whom) – is not surprising.

But Wittgenstein's achievement is many-faceted, and a good deal more extensive that these comments suggest. I have limited myself here to only one of these facets – the doctrine, namely, that people, and especially philosophers, have been led into confusion "by means of language." Although so popular at one time, there is a tendency at

---

[6] Ryle's foreigner at Oxford, for example, who has apparently fallen victim to the fallacy of Composition (i.e., of attributing to the whole – the University – those qualities possessed by its parts). It is surprising how much of Ryle's work, like Wittgenstein's, tends to fall under this category – how much of it, that is to say, can be regarded as an application and exploration of the familiar common fallacies.

[7] See, for example, F. P. Ramsey's charming talk in *The Foundations of Mathematics* (London: Routledge & Kegan Paul Ltd., 1954), "Epilogue," pp. 387–392.

present to reject or, at least, to down-grade this doctrine. I have tried to show here that what is being down-graded is not so much Wittgenstein's version of it, and all that he apparently packed into it, but one a good deal poorer than it.

3

It is possible, however, that Wittgenstein will be remembered, if he is remembered, not for the thesis which forms the theme of this book, but for some of the other matters which play an important role in his works. I have said nothing about them thus far, nor do I wish to do so here. Instead I should like to turn to a certain theme which appears in some of the writings he did very soon after finishing the *Blue Book* – a theme which promises a way out of the dilemma posed by that book.

CHAPTER SIX

PICTURE THEORY IN
WITTGENSTEIN'S LATER PHILOSOPHY

I

In what has preceded we have seen how the diverse literary sources of Wittgenstein's works have been reponsible for the various strains and stresses in it and how these, in turn, have given rise to some of the curious theories associated with linguistic philosophy. But although Wittgenstein managed to reconcile these diverse strains no more success-fully than those who succeeded him, seeing his work against its historical and literary background has enabled us to see better why, in his case, it did not and could not succeed. It also enabled us to see how he might have come to think that he did.

But interestingly enough there appears in the works which immediate-tely followed the *Blue Book* a theory of the functioning of language which, although still very much undeveloped, seems to have all the features of a solution to this problem. This has to do with what Wittgen-stein has to say regarding the way our minds tend to be held captive by "pictures." The view which seems to emerge from these writings is that the mind is held captive and in bondage not by language, pure and simple, but rather by "pictures" which language has a tendency to generate.

It is strange that so little notice has been taken of this theory. But this is perhaps due to the fact that it is a *picture-theory*, and we have become accustomed to thinking that although such a theory figures prominently, indeed, in the *Tractatus*, Wittgenstein gave it up later on. That he gave it up is, of course, true. But it is also true that although Wittgenstein gave up *that* picture theory, he never really gave up trying to develop *a* picture theory, or to explore the earlier one in other directions. This is one of those threads in Wittgenstein's thought which has a tendency to break off at certain points but which somehow never completely vanishes from sight.

2

Now what is it for the mind to be misled or held captive by *pictures*? A
rather striking example of what Wittgenstein had in mind here is to be
found in Norman Malcolm's *Memoir of Wittgenstein*. Malcolm recounts
how:

> At one of the at-homes, Wittgenstein related a riddle for the purpose of throwing
> some light on the nature of philosophy. It went as follows: Suppose that a cord
> was stretched tightly around the earth at the equator. Now suppose that a piece
> one yard long was added to the cord. If the cord was kept taut and circular in
> form, how much above the surface of the earth would it be? Without stopping
> to work it out, everyone present was inclined to say that the distance of the cord
> from the surface of the earth would be so *minute* that it would be imperceptible.
> But this is wrong. The actual distance would be nearly six inches. Wittgenstein
> declared that this is the *kind* of mistake that occurs in philosophy. It consists in
> being *misled by a picture*. In the riddle the picture that misleads us is the com-
> parison of the length of the additional piece with the length of the whole cord.
> But we are misled by it to draw a wrong conclusion. A similar thing happens in
> philosophy: we are constantly deceived by mental pictures which are in them-
> selves correct."[1]

Although very little has so far been made by Wittgenstein scholars
about such remarks concerning the sources and nature of philosophical puzzlement, they present what may yet prove to be some
of Wittgenstein's most fruitful insights. Unfortunately some of his most
enlightening comments on this topic are either buried in the least highly
regarded of his posthumous works – *The Remarks on the Foundations of
Mathematics* – or in manuscripts which have not as yet been published.

Thus, for example, in some unsigned lecture notes appended to a
mimeographed copy of the *Blue Book* in the Hoose Library of Philosophy (at the School of Philosophy, University of Southern California) a
number of remarks are to be found which are for our purposes here
immensely interesting.[2] They are somewhat rough and unfinished but
tend, nevertheless, to clarify (in a way which even the *Blue Book* does
not) what precisely, in his view, is so misleading about the terms in which

---

[1] Pp. 53–54.
[2] Professor Alice Ambrose informs me that these notes, only seventeen pages of which are
on deposit in the Hoose Library, are lecture notes taken down by Professor Margaret Mac-
Donald in the year 1934–35. The whole set of these notes, of which Professor Ambrose has a
copy, runs to about 200 pages. These notes, she further informs me, should not be confused
with a set of notes taken down by herself and Miss Margaret Masterman in 1933–34, and
called by them *The Yellow Book*. These latter notes were taken in the intervals between dic-
tation of *The Blue Book*, when Wittgenstein would talk informally about some matter he had
been dictating about.

certain scientific discoveries are sometimes expressed and who in particular, according to him, tends to be misled by them.

Certain mathematical expressions, he says there, lend themselves easily to misunderstanding, but it is not the *mathematician* who is misled by them. On the contrary, his calculations are entirely unaffected by them. It is different, however, with the philosopher of mathematics, or the man on the street. Their interest in these matters arise, initially, not from anything internal or directly relevant to these investigations but rather from the associations these expressions tend to arouse in their minds. What fascinates them are the pictures which the mathematician's talk about his work tends to conjure up. And these pictures are misleading: they tend to make his work seem more important and more glamorous than it would otherwise seem to be. Now this may not be a bad thing, for without such glamour no one might have become interested in these problems to begin with; they are, however, not what the problems, once begun, are really about. In his own words:

Certain verbal forms are misleading for a time and then cease to be misleading. The idea of Imaginary Numbers, e.g. There may have been something misleading in this when it was first introduced but now it is utterly harmless; it just does not mislead anyone, while to say that the appellation "infinite development" is misleading is correct, though of course it does not mislead anyone in his calculations. It misleads in the idea of what they have done and the consequent interest which people have in certain calculations. The idea of the infinite as something huge does fascinate some people and their interest is due solely to that association, though they probably would not admit it. But that has nothing to do with their calculations. We could, e.g., play chess without the board or chessmen, by description of the moves, etc. I might say that chess would never have been invented apart from the board, figures, etc., and perhaps the connection with the movements of troops in battle. No one would have dreamed of inventing the game as played with pencil and paper. That would be right, but still the game (as played either way) would not be wrong. It is the same with mathematics. There is nothing right or wrong in a calculus, but it is its associations which make it seem worth while. But they are quite different from the calculus. Sometimes the associations are connected with practical applications; sometimes they are not. The association of the infinite is with something huge. Without this association no one would care a damn about the infinite.[3]

---

[3] Lecture Thirteen, dated 5.6.35, p. 10. That so much of what Wittgenstein has to say about "pictures" (in the sense explored here) is embedded in a mathematical context may be due to the fact that his initial inspiration here came from Frege. The reader may find it interesting to compare a number of Wittgenstein's remarks with those that can be found, for example, in Frege's *Foundations of Arithmetic*. The reason why mathematicians, Frege states on p. v of this work (in J. L. Austin's translation, New York: Philosophical Library, 1950), feel so much aversion to philosophical arguments is because of the preponderance in them of psychological methods:

When Stricker, for instance, calls our ideas of number motor phenomena and makes them dependent on muscular sensations, no mathematician can recognize his numbers in such

Wittgenstein might have said that it is the same with philosophy itself. A person's interest in philosophy, he might have said, is initially aroused by his belief and expectation that it will answer such questions as, What is the meaning of life? How did the world begin? Is there a God? and so on. But once such a person begins to study philosophy and to pursue it seriously, he discovers that a good deal of the philosopher's work is occupied with investigating somewhat less glamorous subject-matters, such things as, e.g., the nature of a proposition, negation, words, etc.

> stuff or knows where to begin to tackle such a proposition. An arithmetic founded on muscular sensations would certainly turn out sensational enough, but also every bit as vague as its foundations. No, sensations are absolutely no concern of arithmetic. No more are mental pictures, formed from the amalgamated traces of earlier sense-impressions. ... It may, of course, serve some purpose to investigate the ideas and changes of ideas which occur during the course of mathematical thinking; but psychology should not imagine that it can contribute anything whatever to the foundation of arithmetic. To the mathematician as such these mental pictures, with their origins and their transformations are immaterial. (Pp. v–vi.)

Later on, p. x, Frege argues that one must "never ... ask for the meaning of a word in iso-lation, but only in the context of a proposition" – in the *Philosophical Investigations* I, 49, Wittgenstein mentions his debt to Frege for this idea – for if this rule is not observed "one is almost forced to take as the meaning of words mental pictures or acts of the individual mind," and so offend against the rule "always to separate sharply the psychological from the logical, the subjective from the objective." And on p. 35: "I distinguish what I call objective from what is handeable or spatial or real. The axis of the earth is objective, so is the centre of gravity of the solar system, but I should not call them real in the way the earth itself is real. We often speak of the equator as an *imaginary* line; but it would be wrong to call it an imaginary line in the dyslogistic sense; it was not created by thought as the result of a psychological process, but is only recognized or apprehended by thought." Again on pp. 70–1: "It may be that every word calls up some sort of idea in us, even a word like "only"; but this idea need not correspond to the content of the word; it may be quite different in different men. ... Nor does this happen only in the case of particles. There is not the slightest doubt that we can form no idea of our distance from the sun. For even although we know the rule that we must multiply a measuring rod so and so many times, we still fail in every attempt to construct by its means a picture approximating even faintly to what we want. Yet this is no reason for doubting the correctness of the calculation which established the distance, nor does it prevent us in any way from taking that distance as a fact upon which to base further inferences." And, finally, these last few passages:

> Time and time again we are led by our thought beyond the scope of our imagination, without thereby forfeiting the support we need for our inferences. Even if, as seems to be the case, it is impossible for men such as we are to think without ideas, it is still possible for their connexion with what we are thinking of to be entirely superficial, arbitrary and conventional. That we can form no idea of its content is therefore no reason for denying all meaning to a word, or for excluding it from our vocabulary. We are indeed only im-posed on by the opposite view because we will, when asking for the meaning of a word, consider it in isolation, which leads us to accept an idea as the meaning. Accordingly, any word for which we can find no corresponding mental picture appears to have no content. But we ought always to keep before our eyes a complete proposition. Only in a propo-sition have the words really a meaning. It may be that mental pictures float before us all the while, but these need not correspond to the logical elements in the jugdment. It is enough if the proposition taken as a whole has a sense; it is this that confers on its parts also their content. This observation is destined, I believe, to throw light on a whole series of difficult concepts, among them that of the infinitesimal, and its scope is not restricted to mathematics either. (Pp. 71–2.)

See also pp. 22–3, 28–9 and 33–4.

These things, he may be told, are as important as the others and even directly relevant to them, but, of course, compared to the pictures he has of it, they certainly do not seem so. But obviously if such a person is really to come to understand the importance of such investigations, he will need to be shown how the glamour which he initially attached to the subject was generated and how it has misled him. Wittgenstein does not take this question up in any detail here, but he does begin to do so in another unpublished manuscript.[4]

In order to understand a word, he says in this other work, we must know its use. With a great many words a certain picture represents for us the meaning of the word. This is the case, for example, with the word "chair." Now one of the great benefits this tendency of words to arouse pictures of what they represent has, is that it guarantees that we will all use these words in the same way. In other cases, however, "these pictures are very misleading." An example here is the word "particle" which, unfortunately, "is no longer used in such a way that the picture has any use." For rather than guaranteeing that we will use the word in similar ways, such new uses to which such words are put tend rather to have just the reverse effect. And this will be so whenever the words in question no longer continue to be used by us in their ordinary and familiar ways. Then the words are misleading and understandably so, for the pictures which they arouse lead us to expect the wrong things – and with obvious results.[5]

Obviously several points of importance are involved in these remarks. First of all, he clearly identifies here "meaning" (and even "use") with "picture," and picture here is quite clearly a kind of image in one's mind. In other words, we are dealing here with "pictures" in their literal sense, and the theory is that words not only arouse such pictures in one's mind but that the meaning of a good many of them (as well as their use) may be explained in terms of such a criterion.

But that is not all. For a curious by-product of this tendency to continue to apply standard pictures in situations where they are no longer really appropriate is the sense of amazement this often generates.

[4] Norman Malcolm's *Math Notes*. See especially pp. 62–3 from which the quotations which follow are taken. This book consists of notes by Norman Malcolm of Wittgenstein's lectures in the spring of 1939. Unauthorized copies of these notes were made and put on sale in San Francisco in 1954. No publisher is shown.

[5] And that, of course, is the point of Wittgenstein's remark in the *Blue Book* (referred to earlier in my summary of the book) concerning the perplexity caused by what some "popular scientists" have said about matter and solidity. "Our perplexity," he writes there, "was based on a misunderstanding; the picture of the thinly filled space had been wrongly *applied*. For this picture of the structure of matter was meant to explain the very phenomenon of solidity."

Thus, for example, thinking of the formula "the cardinal number of all cardinal numbers" in terms of, say, "chairs" has a kind of dizzying effect on the mind, for the number involved is truly staggering. It conjures up, he says, "a picture of an *enormous colossal* number. And this picture has a charm." But the imagery here, although a natural and understandable consequence of our tendency to assimilate and correlate various expressions in our language, is entirely inappropriate. For, in fact, we have as yet, as he puts it, "no right to have an image. The imagery is connected with a different calculus: $30 \times 30 = 900$." It is the same in many other cases as well. The sense of amazement and puzzlement experienced at such occasions is simply a product of a mis-applied image.

On the contrary, we may even go further than that. If something about a certain subject or problem "charms or astounds" us, we may conclude from this that it is because we have been captivated by "the wrong imagery." Imagery of that sort is a function of metaphors and such metaphors remain "fishy" as long as they are "exciting." When we begin to see these things in their true light, the amazement and excite-ment simply vanishes. Thus, for example, certain parts of mathematics are regarded as "deep." "But the apparent depth comes from a wrong imagery. It is pedestrian as any calculus." Yet that is precisely the way people were misled about the infinitesimal calculus, when they mistaken-ly believed that it treated of infinitely small quantities. "People said later, "If you look into it, there's nothing infinitely small there." But what did they expect to find; what would it be like for something to be infinitely small? Why are they disappointed? And what do they mean by saying it doesn't treat of the infinitely small? This might be contra-dicted. First, "infinitely small" hasn't a very familiar use. Second, in-stead of saying it doesn't treat of something infinitely small, we should say it doesn't treat of *small* things at all." But it is because we think of such things in terms of such misleading images (in terms, for example, of sizes, as here) that we go so wrong. The amazement and excitement which such things inspire in us should be taken as a sign that we have simply been misled.

Wittgenstein speaks in these manuscripts of "charm," "excitement," "amazement" (just as previously he spoke of "interest" and "fascina-tion") but it is easy to see how these expressions give way in the later works to such more familiar ones as "puzzlement," "wonder," "con-fusion," etc. That transition is to be found, in fact, even in this work itself. On page 6, for example, we find him remarking:

There is one kind of misunderstanding which has a kind of charm ... we say that the line intersects at an imaginary point. This sets the mind in a whirl, and gives a pleasant feeling of paradox, e.g., saying that there are numbers bigger than infinity. ... He has employed a sensational way of expressing what he has discovered, so that it looks like a different *kind* of discovery. ... he describes a new state of affairs in old words, and so we don't understand him. The picture he makes does not lead us on. By the words of ordinary language we conjure up a familiar picture – but we need more than the right picture, we need to know the correct use.

And that is precisely where such new notations, he emphasizes here, fail us so badly. The fact is that "in an overwhelming number of cases people do have the same sort of images suggested by words. This is a mere matter of fact about what happens in our minds, but a fact of enormous importance."[6] In view of this, it is not difficult to see why and how confusions arise. For all that is really necessary for this to happen is for us to use familiar words in unfamiliar ways. The pictures aroused will be correct enough but, of course, they will be misleading. And it is in such misleading pictures, he concludes here, "that most of the problems of philosophy arise."[7]

3

Up to this point I have been concentrating upon these early unpublished works, and we should now turn to those writings that are familiar to us and see whether the emphasis we have given to the passages noted above is sustained by those other works. The fact of course is that not only is this emphasis sustained in these other works but, on the contrary, when read now in the light of this emphasis they tend to take on new meaning and to become still more interesting. As far as the *Blue Book* is concerned, for example, it becomes clear for the first time why so much of it is taken up, as we have seen, with his attack upon the *imagist* Theory of Meaning. Without the background which the remarks noted above provide, that problem there seems somewhat artificial and even academic. And this could be said of a good many other related discussions and observations in the *Blue Book*. Without these further source materials and aids, they seem more like conclusions to discussions than the substance which led to them. No wonder they often seem so

---

[6] *Math Notes*, p. 39.
[7] P. 41. Cf. here *Philosophical Investigations* I, 141: "Can there be a collision between picture and application? There can, inasmuch as the picture makes us expect a different use, because people in general apply *this* picture like *this*."

puzzling. Certainly not everything that is puzzling about them disappears when read in the light of some of this other material. That they
become more immediately intelligible to us in their light there cannot,
I think, be any doubt.

Let me illustrate this with one or two examples.

"The new expression misleads us," he says on p. 23 of the *Blue Book*,
"by calling up pictures and analogies which make it difficult for us to go
through with our conventions. And it is extremely difficult to discard
these pictures unless we are constantly watchful." Now we can be so
watchful, he goes on to tell us there, by asking ourselves at such times,
"*How far does the analogy between these uses go?*" We can also try to
construct, as he says further, "new notations, in order to break the spell
of those which we are accustomed to."[8]

In view of what we have seen Wittgenstein say about "pictures," etc.,
in the other manuscripts, I think we can understand now better than was
possible for us before the deeper implications of these remarks – Why,
for example, he should say that it is extremely difficult to discard these
pictures, How being watchful in the way he there suggests will enable us
to do so, Why he should speak of the whole process in the terms in which
he does ("go through with our conventions," "spell," "notation") etc.
And the same may be said, I believe, of a good many other pages in the
Blue Book.[9]

Although such discussions tend to be more puzzling without these
further aids, occasionally they are, as we can now see, surprisingly explicit and clear. His remark on page 43 is a case in point. "The scrutiny
of the grammar of a word," he says there, summarizing his results,
"weakens the position of certain fixed standards of our expression which
had prevented us from seeing facts with unbiassed eyes. Our investigation tried to remove this bias, which forces us to think that the facts
must conform to certain pictures embedded in our language."

What has been said about the *Blue Book* applies equally well
to the *Brown Book*. The material here, however, is much too extensive
to be noted in any detail. It would in any case be unnecessary to do so,
for a good deal of it contains the same sort of argument already familiar
to us from the *Blue Book*. The most important of this, for our purposes
here, is, again, probably the series of discussions in which he tries to
remove the reader's temptation to believe that images must interpose

---

[8] Cf. here the Remarks on the *Foundations of Mathematics*, p. 61: "... the point of a new
technique of calculation is to supply us with a *new* picture, *a new form of expression*..."

[9] See, for example, his discussions on pp. 36–7 and 39–41.

between us and our various activities.[10] His concern with pictures and images in this sense, although related to the discussions which we have been following here, is already, of course, an extension of them. His best discussion of this problem in the *Brown Book* is probably the long, summary, passage on pp. 165–67 which illustrates rather well the way in which he was beginning to explore some of the wider issues to which, as it seems, his notice of the picture-generating capacity of language led him.

We will be able to "shed light on all these considerations," he states there, if we will compare what really happens when we remember the face of someone who, say, enters our room with what we are often inclined to say happens. Now we are often "obsessed" with the "primitive conception" that what we do here is to compare the man we see with a memory image of him in our mind. We represent "'recognizing someone'," that is, "as a process of identification by means of a picture." Although this may sometimes be the case, often, no such comparison takes place at all. Now it may be that we are tempted to give such a description simply because there are memory images, and very often "such an image comes before our mind immediately *after* having recognized someone," but that is not what generally happens in cases of recognition.[11]

We seem here to be under "the same strange illusion," he says, as we are when, after, for example, "repeating a tune to ourselves and letting it make its full impression on us, we say "This tune says *something*" and then try to find our *what* it says. Or when we say of some tune played that "This is not how it ought to be played, it goes like this," and then go on to whistle it in a different tempo. Now here too, he points out, one is inclined to say "that there *must* be a paradigm somewhere in our mind" and what we do here is to adjust the tempo to that paradigm. But, he points out, "in most cases if someone asked me 'How do you think this melody should be played?,''I will, as an answer, just whistle it in a particular way, and nothing will have been present to my mind but the tune *actually whistled* (not an image of *that*)."

The fact is that all these processes have a greater simplicity and directness about them than our philosophizing about them leads us to believe. "What we call 'understanding a sentence,' for example, 'has, in

---

[10] See, for example, pp. 96, 112–3, 118–9, 125, 130, 139, 142–5, 150–1, 154, 156 and 163.
[11] Cf. here also *Philosophical Investigations* I, 604: "It is easy to have a false picture of the processes called "recognizing"; as if recognizing always consisted in comparing two impressions with one another." Etc.

many cases, a much greater similarity to understanding a musical theme than we might be inclined to think." This doesn't mean that "understanding a musical theme is more like the picture which one tends to make oneself of understanding a sentence; but rather that this picture is wrong, and that understanding a sentence is much more like what really happens when we understand a tune than at first sight appears. For understanding a sentence, we say, points to a reality outside the sentence. Whereas one might say 'Understanding a sentence means getting hold of its content; and the content of the sentence is *in* the sentence'."[12]

Interesting as all this must appear to us and obviously related as it is to some of the things we have noted above, what we have yet to see more clearly is the way Wittgenstein came to connect his thoughts about this picture-generating capacity of language with his later formulation and thoughts on the nature and sources of philosophical confusion. And for this we should now turn to the *Philosophical Investigations*.

If we will recall the importance which Wittgenstein had earlier invested his distinction between meaning and use (identyfiing the former with images in our minds and explaining confusion as the consequence of the failure of these images to keep up with changing usage), then, I think, it will not surprise us to find, again, that one of the major goals of the *Philosophical Investigations* is (as was the case with both the *Blue Book* and the *Brown Book*)that of unseating the view that understanding a word or a sentence means having images of what the words represent flash before our minds.[13]

Now the trouble with this failure of ours "to get away from the idea that using a sentence involves imagining something for every word" is, he argues here, that we do not realize that we do all sorts of things with words – turning "them sometimes into one picture, sometimes into another."[14] Furthermore, such pictures are often "only like an illustration to a story" and from it alone it is mostly impossible "to conclude anything at all" – for only "when one knows the story does one know the significance of the picture."[15] But mainly, of course, the trouble with such pictures is that they seem "to fix the sense *unambiguously*"

---

[12] Cf. here *Philosophical Investigations* I, 396: "It is no more essential to the understanding of a proposition that one should imagine anything in connexion with it, than that one should make a sketch from it."

[13] See, for example, what he says in *Philosophical Investigations* I, 6; and I, 139.

[14] *Philosophical Investigations* I, 449.

[15] *Ibid.*, I, 663.

when this is not at all the case. On the contrary, "the actual use, compared with that suggested by the picture," is "muddied."[16]

Certainly language has this effect on us – "the picture is there"; nor need we necessarily dispute its "validity in any particular case." But we do "want to understand the application of the picture."[17] And not only is this often lacking, but other pernicious effects result as well. Or, as he himself puts it later. "What this language primarily describes is a picture." What is to be done with the picture, how it is to be used, is still obscure. Quite clearly, however, it must be explored if we want to understand the sense of what we are saying. But the picture seems to spare us this work: it already points to a particular use. This is how it takes us in."[18]

In order to save ourselves from being taken in in this way we ought always to ask: does reality accord with such pictures?[19] These pictures *seem* "to determine what we have to do, what to look for, and how" – but they really do not do so. They *seem* "to make the sense of the expressions unmistakable" but in fact prove to be utterly misleading.[20] For example, "What am I believing in when I believe that men have souls? What am I believing in, when I believe that this substance contains two carbon rings? In both cases there is a picture in the foreground, but the sense lies far in the background; that is, the application of the picture is not easy to survey."[21] In ordinary circumstances such words and the pictures which they generate "have an application with which we are familiar. – But if we suppose a case in which this application is absent we become as it were conscious for the first time of the nakedness of the words and the picture,"[22] of how "idle" such pictures are.[23] In the end we must simply regard them as "illustrated turns of speech,"[24] which stand "in the way of our seeing the use of the word as it is."[25]

---

[16] I, 426.
[17] I, 423.
[18] II, vii.
[19] I, 352.
[20] *Ibid.*
[21] I, 422.
[22] I, 349.
[23] I, 291.
[24] I, 295.
[25] I, 305.

4

The theory which Wittgenstein expounds in the *Remarks on the Foundations of Mathematics* (to turn finally to that work) is essentially similar to the one which I have tried to reproduce above from other sources. Some of the points are even expressed in almost identical terms, although not always so explicitly as there. Remark number 17 in Appendix II, for example, is a case in point and should be compared with the similar observation (also dealing with the use of the word "infinite") reproduced earlier from *Math Notes*. It runs as follows:

"Ought the word 'infinite' to be avoided in mathematics?" Yes; where it appears to confer a meaning upon the calculus; instead of getting one from it. This way of talking: "But when one examines the calculus there is nothing infinite there" is of course clumsy. – but it means: is it really necessary here to conjure up the picture of the infinite (of the enormously big)? And how is this picture connected with the *calculus*? For its connexion is not that of the picture IIII with 4. To act as if one were disappointed to have found nothing infinite in the calculus is of course funny; but not to ask: what is the everyday employment of the word "infinite," which gives it its meaning for us; and what is its connexion with these mathematical calculi?

And in this next and final remark in this Appendix, he summarizes his results in these words:

What I am doing is, not to show that calculations are wrong, but to subject the *interest* of calculations to a test. I test, e.g., the justification for still using the word ... here. Or really, I keep on urging such an investigation. I show that there is such an investigation and what there is to investigate there. Thus I must say, not: "We must not express ourselves like this," or "That is absurd," or "That is uninteresting," but: "Test the justification of this expression in this way." You cannot survey the justification of an expression unless you survey its employment; which you cannot do by looking at some facet of its employment, say a picture attaching to it.

This remark is, of course, reminiscent of several other remarks quoted earlier from other sources dealing with this same theme. Throughout many of these remarks Wittgenstein is anxious to put us on our guard against our tendency to be bewitched by pictures which strike our fancy but which on closer inspection have no or extremely weak justification. As he puts it in remark number 16 here:

If the interest here attaches to the proposition that has been proved, then it attaches to a picture which has an extremely weak justification, but which fascinates us by its queerness, like, e.g., the picture of the "direction" of time. It makes one's thoughts reel mildly. Here I can only say: depart as quickly as possible from this picture, and see the interest of this calculation in its application.

That there may be nothing at all trivial in the point Wittgenstein is here urging may perhaps be gathered from a rather recent example – the attempts to make a landing on the moon. Scientists feared that such a landing would prove to be either difficult or impossible because of the thick layer of dust with which they believed the moon was covered. But the belief proved to be a myth. As one scientist connected with the project later remarked: it was an idea, he said, which people simply became *fascinated* with and would not give up, but there was really never any reason to entertain it at all. Wittgenstein has here obviously put his finger on some very deep and pervasive human tendencies, tendencies, obviously, of far-reaching consequences.

In remarks 10, 11 and 12 he offers an extended example of the mechanics of such deceptions. Since his remarks here introduce us again to most of the key terms of the theory "(interest," "mystery," "picture," "excitement," etc.) I will quote them in full before going on to summarize the main issues in my own words.

10. "Fractions cannot be arranged in an order of magnitude." – First and foremost, this sounds extremely interesting and remarkable. It sounds interesting in a quite different way from, say, a proposition of the differential calculus. The difference, I think, resides in the fact that *such* a proposition is easily associated with an application to physics, whereas *this* proposition belongs simply and solely to mathematics, seems to concern as it were the natural history of mathematical objects themselves. One would like to say of it e.g.: it introduces us to the mysteries of the mathematical world. *This* is the aspect against which I want to give a warning. When it looks as if . . ., we should look out.

11. When, on hearing the proposition that the fraction cannot be arranged in a series in order of magnitude, I form the picture of an unending row of things, and between each thing and its neighbour new things appear, and more new ones again between each of these things and its neighbour, and so on without end, then certainly there is something here to make one dizzy. But once we see that this picture, though very exciting, is all the same not appropriate; that we ought not to let ourselves be trapped by the words "series," "order," "exist," and others, we shall fall back on the *technique* of calculating fractions, about which there is no longer anything *queer*. The fact that in a technique of calculating fractions the expression "the next greatest fraction" has no sense, that we have not given it any sense, is nothing to marvel at. If we apply a technique of continuous interpolation of fractions, we shall not be willing to call any fraction the "next biggest."

12. To say that a technique is unlimited does *not* mean that it goes on without ever stopping – that it increases immeasurably; but that it lacks the institution of the end, that it is not finished off. As one can say of a sentence that it is not finished off if it has no period. Or of a playing-field that it is unlimited, when the rules of the game do not prescribe any boundaries – say by means of a line. For the point of a new technique is to supply us with a *new* picture, *a new form of expression*; and there is nothing so absurd as to try and describe this new schema, this new kind of scaffolding, by means of the old expression.

I have been concentrating here entirely on the second Appendix, but these relevant points and issues and their further elaboration are to be found scattered throughout the *Foundations*. In addition to remark number i in this Appendix, the reader may find it valuable to examine the following remarks as well: *Part I*: Nos. 6, 14, 74, 118 and 125. *Part II*: No. 29. *Part III*: Nos. 12 and 21. *Part IV*: Nos. 6, 9, 16, 25, 29 and 37. *Part V*: Nos. 3 and 16.

Wittgenstein's doctrine of pictures, as some of these remarks show, has important and wide-reaching implications for the logic of discovery. Contained in them as well, however, is something that is of even wider significance. It has to do in a way, I believe, with the point long ago expressed by Bishop Butler that everything is what it is and not another thing.[26] Part of the meaning of this remark is, I believe, that everything should be or ought to be evaluated in terms of the categories which it itself brings along. If we are looking at a work of art, for example, we should resist responding or evaluating it in terms of any external interests that it may have for us. A painting may be interesting to us because of the memories of our childhood it may awaken in us, or because an enormous amount of money was spent in purchasing it, or because it is a painting of the artist's son or mistress, but obviously none of these are what makes the painting a good painting – assuming it is a good painting. If these, then, are the reasons we find ourselves aroused, interested and fascinated by the work, we can be certain that it is not to the painting as such that we are responding and that in a sense, therefore, we are misled by our *interest* in it.

The same may be said about our experience in connexion with other matters as well. If, for example, we find ourselves responding with greater interest and enthusiasm to, say, literature than to mathematics, the chances are that our response to the former is of an external sort. For what may make the work of literature more interesting to us are perhaps the characters with which it deals and with whom we have a certain affinity, or their life stories which seem to shed some light on our own, or the generally large doses of sex which we find pleasurably arousing. But these in themselves are not what makes a great work of literature great and worthy of our attention. What makes it great is not

---

[26] This was written before the publication of *Wittgenstein's Lectures and Conversations on Aesthetics, Psychology and Religious Belief* in which I now find this curious (and, of course, gratifying) remark: "Those sentences have the form of persuasion in particular which say 'This is *really* this'. This means there are certain differences which you have been persuaded to neglect. It reminds me of that marvellous motto: 'Everything is what it is and not another thing'." (P. 27.)

its ability to satisfy these diverse, external needs but rather that it is able to exploit to the full its own peculiar medium and to give expression to itself. And in this sense both literature and mathematics – in fact all the arts and sciences – are as one. Each has its own goals and if they succeed in achieving them are as worthy and internally as interesting as any other. If therefore in view of this we find ourselves responding with greater interest to one as opposed to some other art or object, it is not because of anything that particular art or object (say, literature) possesses that the other does not. More likely, it is rather because we are responding to something that is not at all intimately connected with the thing as it is in itself. For from the point of view of the things themselves, they are simply what they are. If, then, one still tends to arouse more interest than some other object – or even, we might say, if one simply does arouse our *interest* – Wittgenstein is perhaps not wrong in urging us to become suspicious and enquire whether perhaps we are not looking at the thing through some misleading picture. Does infinitesimal calculus strike you as being "deep"? It is as "pedestrian" as any calculus, he would reply.

5

In restating, as I have tried to do in this chapter, Wittgenstein's position in terms of this new idea and emphasis, I have, of course, taken some liberties with the order of his own exposition. This has been necessary in order to make it possible for us to look at such remarks in the *Philosophical Investigations* as, for example, "Philosophy is a battle against the bewitchment of our intelligence by means of language";[27] "A simile that has been absorbed into the forms of our language produces a false appearance";[28] "A *picture* held us captive,"[29] in the way in which perhaps we might now look at all Wittgenstein's remarks regarding the genesis of philosophical confusion.

How illuminating this might prove to be we might perhaps gather if we now turned for a moment to that passage in the *Brown Book* which we found so puzzling earlier. The passage appears on pp. 107–8 and has to do with the way in which, according to him, similes and metaphors tend to mislead us.

[27] I, 109.
[28] I, 112.
[29] I, 115.

Certain ideas of the past, the future and the present, he says there, have a "problematic and almost mysterious aspect." "What this aspect is and how it comes about that it appears can be almost characteristically exemplified if we look at the question "Where does the present go when it becomes past, and where is the past?" – Under what circumstances has this question an allurement for us? For under certain circumstances it hasn't, and we should wave it away as nonsense."[30]

The allurement comes from looking at these events, he says, in terms of certain similes which although innocent themselves, are here completely inappropriate and misleading. It is clear, he argues, that this question ("Where does the present go when it becomes past, and where is the past?") "most easily arises if we are preoccupied with cases in which there are things flowing by us, – as logs of wood float down a river. In such a case we can say the logs which *have passed* us are all down towards the left and the logs which *will pass* us are all up towards the right. We then use this situation as a simile for all happening in time and even embody the simile in our language, as when we say that 'the present event passes by' (a log passes by), 'the future event is to come' (a log is to come). We talk about the flow of events; but also about the flow of time – the river on which the logs travel."

What we found so objectionable earlier about this and similar kinds of analysis in his works is that they seemed to attribute the rise of various metaphysical theories, so complex as they often are and supported by such subtle and intricate arguments, to such seemingly absurd and unbelievable causes. Surely, we were inclined to say, it is a wild leap to suggest that Augustine's puzzlement about time arose in this way. On the contrary, to try to dismiss it in such a high-handed manner is itself simply absurd. For, after all, what proof is there that such an analogy even occurred to Augustine during his deliberations on this problem?

But from what has been said here it could perhaps be argued that it is really not Wittgenstein's intention to try to base his case, here or elsewhere, on any such claims. His point seems rather to be that our questions and puzzlement (whether it is about time or anything else) is often a product of our tendency to look at these things through misleading pictures (whatever these may be at any one occasion or for anyone particular philosopher). On the other hand, if he intended to be any more specific than this, then the whole question simply becomes an empirical one. To settle it we would need to ask people whether, for

---

[30] Notice here, of course, the words "mysterious," "allurement."

example, in thinking about the flow of time they had in their minds, however vaguely, some notion (as he seems to suggest in the *Brown Book* that they do) of the flow of logs down a river. We might by investigating it in this way perhaps discover that either they had something else in the back of their minds (must is be *logs*? Could it not be, perhaps, clouds floating across the sky?) or, more probably, nothing at all. But this is probably not what Wittgenstein had in mind here. His point seems rather to be that the general tendency of language is to generate pictures in our minds (this is a fact of language and is essential to his case) and that this cannot fail to have an adverse effect upon philosophy – such pictures being often incongruent with the facts which they are designed to explain, must prove misleading. Certainly they make, as we must all see, the philosopher's task more difficult.

It is perhaps this general fact about language (and not any one particular picture which he need necessarily defend) that he seems mainly to base his case upon. This is what, for example, his remarks about "symbolism" seem to entail. "Thus it can come about," as he puts it here, "that we aren't able to rid ourselves of the implications of our symbolism." We become "obsessed" with it – an analogy which "irresistibly drags us on," leads us into confusion, etc.[31]

The "symbolism" or "ideography" of which he speaks here is obviously of a much more complicated kind than the one discussed in the *Tractatus*. But like it, it is designed to show how language by failing to be congruent with the states of affairs it is designed to depict, gives rise to difficulties. Both doctrines, that is to say, are designated to be descriptive of certain very general and universal aspects of the operation of language. Unfortunately, his tendency to talk at such great length and with so much detail about "particular cases" tends to obscure this.

6

Wittgenstein's later theory of pictures is interesting to us for more than one reason.

For one thing it suggests, it seems to me, a possible way out of the difficulties raised in earlier chapters about his general position. As we saw there one of the main difficulties of Wittgenstein's theory is that, unlike its parallel theory in Kant, it doesn't really succeed in explaining why language tends to have such a dominating and perverse effect upon

31 Cf. here *Philosophical Investigations* I, 140 where he couples 'pictures' with 'analogy.'

us. What it seems to lack is convincing arguments or answers as to how language manages to exercise such a tyrannically bewitching power over our minds and what about it enables it to continue to deceive us even when its deceptions are brought to light and exposed. As pointed out there, while the Kantian formulation of this problem, dealing as it does, with some of the fundamental patterns of our thought, carries conviction, Wittgenstein's reduction of it turns out to be unbelievable. And what it lacks mostly is, of course, that universality and transcendentalism that is so much a part of Kant's doctrine and analysis. For with Kant, as was pointed out, it is not a matter of any one particular syllogism leading us to draw a false inference. His doctrine of transcendental illusions is not derived in any such way; on the contrary, any syllogism at all could serve as an illustration, for it is the form of the syllogism (expressive as that is of the pattern of our thought) which gives rise to such illusions, and not its matter. No particular example need therefore be especially defended or regarded as preeminent – some universal feature concerning the operation of our minds guarantees that the facts are as stated, and inevitably so. But in Wittgenstein the matter seems entirely reversed. His dialectic, which lacks this kind of built-in guarantee or transcendentalism, seems always in need of further and further support, each time requiring to be proven anew. His examples, as a result, assume enormous importance, each becoming a kind of test-case of his entire argument. This is probably why, as pointed out above, no example really pleased him. As we can now see better perhaps, in the absence of this universal feature, none really could.

But I think we can now see also that what Wittgenstein seemed to lack before is made up here by his doctrine of pictures. For this tendency of language to generate pictures is not only something universal about language but may very well be conceived as precisely the sort of fault in it, that his theory here requires. Thus, he might well have argued, like Kant before him, that it is not any particular misleading analogy or metaphor that creates the "grammatical illusions" which are responsible for philosophical puzzlement and confusion, but this transcendental aspect of language which brings it about and is responsible for it. It is for this reason, similarly, that no particular example is necessarily decisive. Each, however, because it tends to reflect that basic trouble at the core of language, can be taken as evidence of it.

Wittgenstein's doctrine of pictures, like so much else in his work is, of course, in need of development and exploration. What we find in his works is simply scattered hints and observations. Nor are these here

necessarily damaging to the metaphysician whose work they are designed, here as elsewhere, to unmask and illuminate.

For even granting this feature about language, it does not necessarily
follow that metaphysicians have in fact been taken in by it and that
their strange talk is a sign of this. For after all is it not still possible that
these strange things which they are in the habit of saying are really
attempts on their part to generate new pictures, to break the spell which
the old ones exercise over us, etc.? Is this not, after all, what everyone
is compelled to do when he wishes to communicate something new and
different to another person? The only tool such a person has are the
ordinary words of our language and these words already have their
meanings. If he is to succeed in doing what he sets out to do, assuming
that he really has something new to communicate, he will be compelled
to try to revise these meanings, to stretch them, even to play havoc with
them. For what else can he do? The ordinary man, of course, rarely
attempts this but this is because he rarely has anything new to say.

But it is obviously different with the metaphysician, or, for that
matter, with any reflective person. With them it is indeed a battle
against the bewitchment of their intelligence by means of language, for
to them ordinary language is confining and inadequate and does not,
as they see it, do justice to the complexity and unique character of their
experience, whatever that may be. If, in view of this, they should
suddenly begin to speak in what appears to us to be a strange tongue,
what force can there be to the suggestion that they have been taken in
by language?

But Wittgenstein has no doubt put his finger on a certain difficulty
here – one peculiar, however, not so much to the metaphysician but to
the student of metaphysics. For the problems which confront him
whenever he attempts to come to terms with a metaphysical work are
truly enormous. His only guide in trying to grapple with a philosophical
text are the words on the printed page and these words tend, naturally,
to repeat to him their old stories. If he is to gather what the metaphysician really wishes to convey to him he must try to resist the old
associations which these words arouse in him and try, rather, to make
himself receptive to the new meanings the metaphysician has invested
these words and the new impressions he hopes they will make on him.
That what makes this task difficult and liable to all sorts of confusion
are the old pictures associated with these words there probably is no
doubt. That metaphysical works should lend themselves so easily to
such misunderstandings and misinterpretations is also no doubt true.

Certainly a good deal of its apparent oddness can be explained in this way.

In all this, therefore, Wittgenstein is no doubt right, and in calling our attention to it he has done metaphysics a service. One is now likely to approach a metaphysical text with a good deal more sympathy, patience and understanding. His theory of pictures helps us see, in a way perhaps we had not seen before, why metaphysical texts are so difficult and confusing. This is, of course, far from what he himself had in mind. But for those who are not about to give up metaphysics this is probably its most useful lesson.

It may not, however, be the only one. His notice of this feature of language, so easily missed because it is so simple and obvious, is certainly worthy of being investigated more closely. What its implications may prove to be not only for philosophy of language but for such distant and seemingly unrelated fields as, for example, sociology, politics and psychiatry can only be guessed at. Nor is this the right place to attempt this. Yet it is hard not to notice that the distortions suffered in mental illness and those which are current in politics and which often, whether accidentally or by design, possess entire populations may all be somehow related to the effect which the pictures generated by words and their power to inflame the mind have on it. Certainly words alone have no such motive power. Pictures and their associations might well have.

CHAPTER SEVEN

WITTGENSTEIN AND OUR PHILOSOPHIC TRADITION

Although Wittgenstein's so-called "later philosophy" began, as we have seen, somewhat inauspiciously, it nevertheless contained and went on to explore ideas of great promise. In what has just preceded I have tried to uncover the wider significance and inherent interest of one or two of the more neglected of these ideas and insights. Without trying to add to them further here I should like, in this final chapter, to define what I believe is their over-all *tendency*, and I should like to do this by viewing them in the larger context of our philosophic tradition. To put it briefly, what I should like to do is to consider whether Wittgenstein's later linguistic philosophy does not after all, despite all that has been said about it by both its friends and foes, form as integral a part of our philosophic tradition as, say, Existentialism.

I have purposely chosen to compare it with this other great contemporary philosophical movement, for opponents of linguistic philosophy have sometimes charged that whereas existentialism is a philosophical tendency lying within the great mainstream of western philosophy and very much a part of its great tradition, Wittgenstein's philosophy and the philosophies it has inspired not only are *not* part of this tradition but are even fiercely opposed to it. I wonder, however, whether a good case could not be made out for saying just the reverse of this. In what follows I should like to try to do so. I should like to show, first of all, that there is indeed a good deal of truth to the claim that a certain brand of existentialism has always been present in philosophy; secondly, that although from this point of view Wittgenstein may certainly be regarded as a type of existentialist philosopher, it is an "Existentialism" which points in a distinctly different direction from that of its present-day form; and thirdly and finally, that unlike its present-day form, the direction it points to can, in retrospect, be seen to lie, much more so in fact than existentialism, in the direct line of development of western philosophy.

I

> "The great problem round which everything that I
> write turns is: Is there an order in the world *a priori*,
> and if so what does it consist in?" *Wittgenstein's Note-
> books*, p. 53.

If there is any one concept which is the common property of Existentialists, it is probably the concept of the Absurd. This is not to say that
all Existentialists make use of this concept, or that those who do, mean
the same thing by it. Still if the label "Existentialist" has any meaning
at all and if Existentialists may be said to share anything at all in
common, it is probably the desire to throw some light upon our feeling
of the Absurd – whether they all do call it that or not.

None of them, as far as I know, have said that this feeling of the
Absurd arises from the realization that the world as it appears to us is
somehow other than what it is in itself (which I take to be the theme
round which all philosophy turns) nor have they occupied themselves
with trying to convey their thought in precisely these terms. They have,
however, said such things as the following: that things simply are without having a sufficient reason for being as they are and not otherwise;
that we inhabit an alien world in which human values can have no
foothold; that we live in a senseless world of which we futilely try to
make sense – and that realizing all this gives rise to anguish and despair,
and so on. These are views which, I believe, have been held by all the
great philosophers of the past. They are also, I believe, essentially
similar to those held by Wittgenstein as well. "The sense of the world,"
he says in the *Tractatus*, "must lie outside the world." For "in the world,"
as he goes on to say there, "everything is as it is, and everything
happens as it does happen: *in* it no value exists – and if it did, it would
have no value." For "if there is any value that does have value, it must
lie outside the whole sphere of what happens and is the case. For all that
happens and is the case is accidental. What makes it non-accidental
cannot lie *within* the world, since if it did it would itself be accidental. It
must lie outside the world." This being so – the world being accidental,
arbitrary, and beyond good and evil – "it is impossible," he concludes
"for there to be propositions of ethics."[1]

Wittgenstein's handling of this concept of the Absurd is of course

---

[1] *Tractatus Logico-Philosophicus*, translated by D. F. Pears and B. F. Mc Guinness. (London:
Routledge & Kegan Paul, 1961), 6.41–6.42.

different from that of his predecessors, but not unrecognizably so. Although, that is to say, he does not speak of the world being a "shadow" of itself (as Plato does), or of it being his "idea" (as Schopenhauer does), or a product of our "imagination" (as Spinoza does), or of the "categories" (as Kant does), yet what he says about our conceptual system (or "net") which we use in order to make sense of it, seems to amount to very much the same thing. For like Plato, Schopenhauer, Spinoza and Kant, he too seems to have believed that the sort of world we are able to experience, depends very much on the conceptual system we use in organizing it for ourselves and that here too therefore we are under a kind of human and universal deception. In stressing this aspect of our human condition (an aspect which in its modern version is the all-embracing theme of Existentialism) Wittgenstein shows himself to be part of this great philosophical or metaphysical tradition. It is a tradition to which he himself added a memorable chapter – his account in the *Philosophical Investigations* of the games people play. Like Plato's Parable of the Cave as described in the *Republic* and Spinoza's account in his Appendix to Part I of the *Ethics* regarding the common man's worship of God, this chapter is a study in the Absurd. That, at least, is the existential thread which runs through and the concept which seems to inspire and give shape to these three different studies. I shall take them up in turn.

As an illustration of the degrees in which our nature may be enlightened or unenlightened, imagine, Plato says in the *Republic*, the condition of men imprisoned in a dark and deep underground cave. They are chained to their seats and are able to move neither to the right nor to the left. They have been there from birth and sit facing the wall of the cave. It is a deep cave and the long winding entrance to the back of them permits no light to enter. Behind them, somewhat further back, there is a wall or partition, and behind this wall, a path or track. Further back still a fire is burning. Along this track people walk to and fro, carrying all sorts of objects (figures of men, animals, and so on) which project above the partition. As they walk by, some talking some silent, the fire casts shadows of these figurines onto the wall of the cave facing the prisoners. But the prisoners, like their modern counterparts in movie theatres, see neither the fire nor, of course, the men who carry these objects whose shadows are reflected on the wall of the cave. They see only these shadows on the wall. They are aware of nothing else. But concerning these shadows which they see, and which they take to be real things, and the echoes which they hear, they form, after perhaps much trial and error, various theories, some, as we might suppose, highly ingenious – perhaps, that these activities of which they are spectators generally last for periods of some eight hours a day, and only five days of the week. To this knowledge they add, in the course of time, further bits of insight, and thus they pass their existence, the only one they know.

But now suppose, says Plato, we released one of these prisoners and brought him to the rear of the cave. He sees the wall and the track . . . the fire burning in the distance . . . the people and the objects which they carry . . . and he sees the prisoners sitting below watching the shadows.

Not accustomed to such intense light he shuts his eyes, in pain and disbelief. He is seized with fear and is overcome by an urge to return to the more familiar and comfortable condition of the darkness of the cave. In time, however, his eyes become accustomed to the sight and he comes to see that what he once took to be real things were indeed only shadows, and an intense desire possesses him to return to the cave to tell the others what he had seen.

And suppose we now follow him there. These other prisoners have seen neither the wall, nor the men, nor the fire. They see him descending into the cave, falling and stumbling, for the cave is dark and it is difficult for him to find his way about. They laugh and jeer at him, for his movements are absurd. "He has gone up," they say, "only to come back with his sight ruined." He begins, however, to tell them about the great fire burning above and about the partition and the statues and the other things he has seen, but it sounds absurd to them. Obviously it is not worth one's while, they say, even to attempt the ascent. But he is undaunted and persists in enlightening them. They become annoyed and their laughter now turns to anger. They instruct him to keep his peace and not disturb them, or else they themselves will silence him.

And that, concludes Plato, with obvious allusions to Socrates, is what they will do should an opportunity present itself.

This parable, is Plato's way of expressing his belief that the world may, for all we know, be quite other than what it appears to be – that with regard to it we are or may be in a state of human and universal deception. Although this thought, embedded as it is in a parable, can carry us only a little distance, it is in its own way both illuminating and profound. For no doubt other thinkers before Plato had also raised such doubts about our world and entertained such other possibilities, but probably never is such a simple and profound way. For there is a great difference between entertaining possibilities and bringing home to one in such a direct and fundamental way how everything although perfectly consistent with itself may yet be quite other than it appears to be. But although Plato's parable does this, it does not try to say anything (at least in the context of the parable itself) about how this illusion is created or what lies behind it. Although it manages to shake our faith in things as they are, it does so only in an abstract and meta- phorical way. It tells a story and this story has a moral, but how this moral is to be applied in a particular case is not revealed by it. Still it states the problem clearly enough: for if it is indeed true that the world is other than what it appears to be, then not only is it absurd that it should appear as it does and not as it is, but it is also absurd that it should produce the appearances which it does – so absurdly incongruent as they are with their realities.

But so much for Plato and this metaphysical delusion which is peculiar to our condition. When we turn to Spinoza, who is mainly interested in religion and morality, we are confronted with a different kind of delusion and a different kind of absurdity.

After describing in his *Ethics* what he believes to be the nature of God, the manner of his operation, its effect upon the world and man – things so very obvious, at least as he sees them – Spinoza goes on to tell the reader here what it is that may prevent him from seeing these facts as he does. It has to do, he says, with our human-all-too-human belief in the purposiveness of Nature. Why, he asks, are people so prone to believe this about Nature? What is it that stands in their way of see- ing that the facts are quite the contrary, namely, that "nature has no particular goal in view" and that everything in it "proceeds from a sort of necessity, and with the utmost perfection."[2]

Partly, he answers, it is due to ignorance of natural causes, and partly to the all-too-human propensity to seek and believe only that which is useful to us. "Herefrom it follows, first, that men think themselves free inasmuch as they are conscious of their volitions and desires, and never even dream, in their ignorance, of the causes which have disposed them so to wish and desire. Secondly, that men do all things for an end, namely for that which is useful to them, and which they seek" and that Nature too behaves similarity.[3]

---

[2] *The Chief Works of Benedict De Spinoza*, translated by R. H. M. Elwes. (New York; Dover Publications, Inc., 1951), Vol. II, p. 77.

[3] P. 75.

Thus it comes to pass that they only look for a knowledge of the final causes of events, and when these are learned, they are content, as having no cause for further doubt. If they cannot learn such causes from external sources, they are compelled to turn to considering themselves, and reflecting what end would have induced them personally to bring about the given event, and thus they necessarily judge other natures by their own. Further, as they find in themselves and outside themselves many means which assist them not a little in their search for what is useful, for instance, eyes for seeing, teeth for chewing, herbs and animals for yielding food, the sun for giving light, the sea for breeding fish, etc., they come to look on the whole of nature as a means for obtaining such conveniences. Now as they are aware, that they found these conveniences and did not make them, they think they have cause for believing, that some other being has made them for their use. As they look upon things as means, they cannot believe them to be self-created; but, judging from the means they are accustomed to prepare for themselves, they are bound to believe in some ruler or rulers of the universe endowed with human freedom, who have arranged and adapted everything for human use. They are bound to estimate the nature of such rulers (having no information on the subject) in accordance with their own nature, and therefore they assert that the gods ordained everything for the use of man, in order to bind man to themselves and obtain from him the highest honor. Hence also it follows, that everyone thought out for himself, according to his abilities, a different way of worshipping God, so that God might love him more than his fellows, and direct the whole course of nature for the satisfaction of his blind cupidity and insatiable avarice.[4]

"Thus the prejudice," Spinoza concludes this brief history of natural religion, "developed into superstition, and took deep root in the human mind; and for this reason everyone strove zealously to understand and explain the final causes of things; but in their endeavor to show that nature does nothing in vain, i.e., nothing which is useless to man, they only seem to have demonstrated that nature, the gods, and men are all mad together."[5] Consider, he urges, the result.

Among the many helps of nature they were bound to find hindrances, such as storms, earthquakes, diseases, etc: so they declared that such things happen, because the gods are angry at some wrong done them by men, or at some fault committed in their worship. Experience day by day protested and showed by infinite examples, that good and evil fortunes fall to the lot of pious and impious alike; still they would not abandon their inveterate prejudice, for it was more easy for them to class such contradictions among other unknown things of whose use they were ignorant, and thus retain their actual and innate condition of ignorance, than to destroy the whole fabric of their reasoning and start afresh. They therefore laid down as an axiom [deserting in the process the very principle with which they began] that God's judgment far transcends human understanding.[6]

Spinoza's Appendix to Part I of the *Ethics* does not end here. There is no need, however, to relate the contents of the rest of the section: its

[4] Pp. 75–6.
[5] P. 76.
[6] Pp. 76–7.

doctrines – that "final causes are mere human figments," "that everyone judges of things according to the state of his brain," that names may be names of nothing at all, and so on – are all well-known. But the section is interesting not only because of the nature of its doctrines (important as these are) but also because of the effect which their exposition is designed to have upon the mind of the reader. And this effect is that of deflation and disillusionment. Like Plato before him and, as we will see in a moment, Wittgenstein after him, the task which Spinoza has here set himself is to free the mind from the pictures and illusions which have captivated it and hold it in bondage. It is an attempt to show that the world as we tend to experience it is very much a product of our own making, that as such and in itself, stripped of the illusions and deceptions prone to our ways of comprehending it, it is absurdly other than what we are inclined to take it to be.

It would take us too far afield to try to investigate or compare here the kind of implications for life, morality or religion which Plato or Spinoza felt this view of the state of things tends to contain within it. Needless to say, the bulk of their philosophy is concerned with these questions. And this is where, perhaps, Linguistic Philosophy does differ both from traditional philosophy and Existentialism. For unlike both, Linguistic Philosophy although enormously preoccupied with the nature and manner of operation of these illusions, is significantly silent regarding their implications for life and morality. Existentialism, on the other hand, has often been more preoccupied in investigating these implications than in exploring their metaphysical foundations.

In any case, it is with what we might call, strictly intellectual illusions, that the later writings of Wittgenstein are mainly concerned. Nor is this emphasis entirely new, although it may appear so. It is already to be found in Kant, as Schopenhauer quite clearly saw. As the following passages indicate, Schopenhauer might even have recognized its existence in Spinoza, where it is already implicit. "If we want to understand Nature's proceeding," Schopenhauer writes in his book, *The Will in Nature,* "we must not try to do it by comparing her works with her own."

The real essence of every animal form, is an act of the will outside representation, consequently outside its form of Space and Time also; which act, just on that account, knows neither sequence nor juxtaposition, but has, on the contrary, the most indivisible unity. But when our cerebral perception comprehends that form, and still more when its inside is dissected by the anatomical knife, then that which originally and in itself was foreign to knowledge and its laws, is brought under the light of knowledge; but then also, it has to present itself in conformity with the laws and forms of knowledge. The original unity and indivisibility of that act of the will, of that truly metaphysical being, then appears divided into parts lying side by side and functions following one upon another, which all nevertheless present themselves as connected together in closest relationship one to another for mutual help and support, as means and ends one to the other. The understanding, in thus apprehending these things, now perceives the original unity re-establishing itself out of a multiplicity which its own form of knowledge had first brought about, and involuntarily taking for granted that its own way of perceiving this is the way in which this animal form comes into being, it is now struck with admiration for the profound wisdom with which those parts are arranged, those functions combined.

"This is the meaning," Schopenhauer continues, "of Kant's great doctrine, that Teleology is brought into Nature by our own understanding, which accordingly wonders at a miracle of its own creation."

If I may use a trivial simile to elucidate so sublime a matter, this astonishment very much resembles that of our understanding when it discovers that all multiples of 9, when their single figures are added together, give as their product either the number 9 or one whose single figures again make 9; yet it is that very understanding itself which has prepared for itself this surprise in the decimal system.[7]

In his major work, *The World as Will and Idea*, Schopenhauer puts this even better:

The astounding amazement which is wont to take possession of us when we consider the endless design displayed in the construction of organized beings ultimately rests upon the certainly natural but yet false assumption that that *adaption* of the parts to each other, to the whole of the organism and to its aims in the external world, as we comprehend it and judge of it by means of *knowledge*, thus upon the path of the *idea*, has also come into being upon the same path; thus that as it exists *for* the intellect, it was also brought about *by* the intellect. We certainly can only bring about something regular and conforming to law, such, for example, as every crystal is, under the guidance of the law and the rule; and in the same way, we can only bring about something designed under the guidance of the conception of the end; but we are by no means justified in imputing this limitation of ours to nature, which is itself prior to all intellect, and whose action is entirely different in kind from ours.[8]

Using two striking similes, he goes on to point out there the kind of absurdities we fall into when we forget this simple lesson.

If direct insight into the working of nature was possible for us; we would necessarily recognize that the wonder excited by teleology referred to above is analogous to that which that savage[9] referred to by Kant in his explanation of the ludicrous

[7] Translated by K. Hillebrand. (London: George Bell and Sons, 1889), pp. 279–80.

[8] Translated by R. B. Haldane and J. Kemp. 3 vols. (London: Routledge & Kegan Paul, 1883), Vol. III, pp. 76–7.

[9] Cf. here Wittgenstein's remark in the *Philosophical Investigations*, translated by G. E. M. Anscombe. (Oxford: Basil Blackwell, 1953), Part I, Section 194: "When does one have the

felt when he saw the froth irresistibly foaming out of a bottle of beer which had just been opened, and expressed his wonder not that it should come out, but that any one had ever been able to get it in; for we also assume that the teleology of natural productions has been put in the same as it comes out for us. Therefore our astonishment at design may likewise be compared to that which the first productions of the art of printing excited in those who considered them under the supposition that they were works of the pen, and therefore had to resort to the assumption of the assistance of a devil in order to explain them. For, let it be said again, it is our intellect which by means of its own forms ... which first produces the multiplicity and diversity of the parts, and is then struck with amazement at their perfect agreement and conspiring together, which proceeds from the original unity; whereby then, in a certain sense, it marvels at its own work.[10]

Some of these examples might easily have come from the pages of Wittgenstein. As I have already pointed out, a closely parallel one does in fact occur in one of his writings. One example, of course, does not add up to a theory, and Wittgenstein does have a theory about such illusions.

Now the illusions with which he deals in the passages I now wish to consider have to do with our belief in Essences – our tendency to think that there must be something in common among all the members of a class of things called by the same name. It is the kind of tendency to which, for example, Socrates apparently was especially prone. In the *Meno*, for example, he asks: "What is this thing which is called 'shape'? ... Don't you see that I am looking for what is the same in all of them? ... What is it that is common to roundness and straightness and the other things which you call shapes?"[11] Clear and as natural as that kind of question must once have appeared, Wittgenstein would have us see that that is really a "complex question." For why should we assume, as he would ask, that there is such one common property or essence which runs through all such things? Surely, he would say, until we have settled that things share such common properties it makes no sense to ask for them. Such questions are impossible to answer and produce puzzlement (not despair) because they are often impossible questions. They keep the mind, as he puts it in his *Blue and Brown Books*, "pressing against a blank wall, thereby preventing it from ever finding the outlet. To show a man how to get out you have first of all to free him from the misleading influence of the question."[12]

thought: the possible movements of a machine are already there in it in some mysterious sense? – Well, when one is doing philosophy. And what leads us into thinking that? The kind of way in which we talk about machines. ... When we do philosophy we are like savages, primitive people, who hear the expressions of civilized men, put a false interpretation on them, and then draw the queerest conclusions from it."

[10] III, 78–9.
[11] Translated by W. K. C. Guthrie. (Baltimore, Md.: Penguin Books, Inc., 1956), 74D–75A.
[12] (Oxford: Basil Blackwell, 1960), p. 169.

"Instead of producing something common," Wittgenstein explains in *Philosophical Investigations*, "I am saying that these phenomena have no one thing in common which makes us use the same word for all, – but that they are *related* one another in many different ways. And it is because of this relationship, or these relationships, that we call them all [by the same name]. I will try to explain this."

Consider for example the proceeding that we call "games," I mean board-games, card-games, ball-games, Olympic games, and so on. What is common to them all? – Don't say: There *must* be something common, or they would not be called 'games'" – but *look and see* whether there is anything common to all. – For if you look at them you will not see something that is common to *all*, but similarities, relationships, and a whole series of them at that. To repeat: Don't think, but look! – Look for example at board-games, with their multifarious relationships. Now pass to card-games; here you find many correspondences with the first group, but many common features drop out, and others appear. When we pass next to ball-games, much that is common is retained, but much is lost. – Are they all "amusing"? Compare chess with noughts and crosses.
Or is there always winning and losing, or competition between players? Think of patience ... we can go through the many, many other groups of games in the same way; can see how similarities crop up and disappear.
I can think of no better expression to characterize these similarities than "family resemblance"; for the various resemblances between members of a family: build, features, colour of eyes, gait, temperament, etc. etc. overlap and criss-cross in the same way. – ... "games" form a family.
The kinds of number form a family in the same way. Why do we call something a "number"? Well, perhaps because it has a – direct – relationship with several things that have hitherto been called number; and this can be said to give it an indirect relationship to other things we call the same name. And we extend our concept of number as in spinning a thread we twist fibre on fibre. And the strength of the thread does not reside in the fact that some one fibre runs through its whole length, but in the overlapping of many fibres.
But if someone wished to say: "There is something common to all these constructions – namely the disjunction of all their common properties" – I should reply: Now you are only playing with words. One might as well say: "Something runs through the whole thread – namely the continuous overlapping of those fibres.
I *can* give the concept "number" rigid limits ... but I can also use it so that the extension of the concept is *not* closed by a frontier. And this is how we do use the word "game." For how is the concept of a game bounded? What still counts as a game and what no longer does? Can you give the boundary? No. You can *draw* one; for none has so far been drawn.
"But then the use of the word is unregulated, the 'game' we play with it is unregulated." – It is not everywhere circumscribed by rules; but no more are there rules for how high one throws the ball in tennis, or how hard; yet tennis is a game for all that and has rules too.[13]

It would be a mistake to think that Wittgenstein is interested here in merely unseating or unmasking Essentialism. Nor is he merely trying

[13] I, 65–68.

to point out that such questions as, for example, What are games? What is beauty? Justice? and so on are really "loaded" questions, which need themselves to be questioned before they are answered. For what he is interested in showing us is not that there are no such essences to be found, but rather what this search for them, invited as it is by such questions, tends to do to us. For this desire for unity and this will to system, which such questions illustrate and invite, blunts and blinds our perceptions and sensitivities. It does violence to the multifarious nature of our experience, makes it easy for us to ignore what is exceptional in that experience and leads us to take a contemptuous attitude to what is unique and individual in it. In other words, it tends to produce the illusions that the world really is as we have parcelled it out by means of our concepts; that our conceptual net has really caught all there is to catch and nothing at all has gotten away. But how can we be sure of this? Perhaps some fish have not been caught and those that have, are not at all representative of what there is to catch?

2

I said ealier that I thought the leading and dominant idea round which all philosophy turns is this insight regarding the existence of two worlds – the world of Reality and the world of Appearance, the world as it is in itself, and the world as it appears to us. Although only the passages which I quoted from Plato seem to deal directly with this question, I think we can see that in dealing with our conceptual frameworks in the way Wittgenstein and the other philosophers do, they too are very much involved in the same endeavor. For like Plato before them, what they are saying is that the sort of world we are able to experience depends very much on the conceptual system we use in organizing it for ourselves, and that in regard to it, therefore, we must consider ourselves under a kind of human and universal deception. And that I believe is the main moral which Plato's parable, as well as the rest of western philosophy, has as its main object and design.

I do not wish to imply here that all the great philosophers are unanimous on this question. They are not. But what divides them are not goals but means. In these goals they are remarkably at one. They do not, however, always agree as to what constitutes the best methods of arriving at these goals. Another way of putting this would be to say that they agree in their conclusions but not in the proofs that have been provided for them. And on these proofs philosophers are still at work.

It is I think the same with both Existentialism and Linguistic Philosophy. In their basic endeavor – which is to open people's eyes to their true condition – they are at one, as a quick comparison of the views expressed on these matters by each of the founders of these two movements reveals.

Thus in this Introduction to his translation of Kierkegaard's book *Purity of Heart*, we find Douglas Steere summing up Kierkegaard's purpose and achievement in these words: "Kierkegaard conceived it his function as a writer to strip men of their disguises, to compel them to see evasions for what they are, to label blind alleys, to cut off men's retreats, ... to isolate men from the crowd, to enforce self communication, and to bring them solitary and alone before the Eternal. Here he left them. For here that in man which makes him a responsible individual must itself act or it must take flight. No other can make this decision. Only when man is alone can he face the Eternal."[14]

As for Wittgenstein, the proper task of philosophy, he says in the *Philosophical Investigations*, is to uncover "one or another piece of plain nonsense and of bumps that the understanding has got by running its head against the limits of language" (I, 119); its aim is "to teach you to pass from a piece of disguised nonsense to something that is patent nonsense" (I, 464); it is in this way that we can destroy the "houses of cards" and clear up "the grounds of language on which they stand" (I, 113). The end result of this will be that our problems will *"completely* disappear" (I, 113) – for if the aim has been reached, "everything lies open to view and there is nothing to explain" (I, 126).

Their differences are, however, no less illuminating. They differ, we might say, in that one seems to be concerned with what we might call man's psychological and moral condition, while the other is concerned with his intellectual and scientific condition. And this shows through the vocabularies of their respective disciplines. Thus, one speaks of absurdity, the other of nonsense; one speaks of despair, the other of confusion; one speaks of anguish, the other of puzzlement; one speaks of roles we play, the other of games we play; one speaks of shipwreck, the other of not knowing one's way about; and so on. Absurdity, despair, anguish, roles and shipwreck are terms expressive of our psychological and moral states; their intellectual correlatives are nonsense, confusion, puzzlement, games, etc. Even their vocabularies, therefore cannot hide

---

[14] (New York: Harper & Row, Publishers, Inc., 1938), p. 16.

their family resemblance. But if their vocabularies disclose this, they also disclose a decisive separation. What this is, and what it implies is what I now wish to consider.

3

Although such parallels as I have tried to draw the reader's attention to may be acknowledge, it may still be argued that although Existentialism and Linguistic Philosophy are alike in being involved in this great program – alike, that is, in exploring these "troubles in our thoughts" caused by our attempts to make sense of a senseless world – in interpreting these troubles in the psychological and human terms in which it does, Existentialism certainly seems more involved in it than Linguistic Philosophy, whose tendency is to become more and more scientific, and with this seemingly more and more trivial.

It is both strange and ironic that this should seem so, for in a sense it could be said that of the two, Existentialism is a good deal closer to science and its methods and more science-like than Linguistic Philosophy. On the contrary, in dealing with these problems in the way it does, it may be said that it has failed to share in certain fruits, the labors of which have been carried on in philosophy for some two or three hundred years now. To see this we have to consider some of the facets of the history of this struggle.

Although this struggle begins properly with Locke, its seed has been present in philosophy from its very beginnings. Thus, we might say, that in trying to shake our faith in things as they appear to us, to plant a seed of doubt in our minds, to make us aware of other possibilities, philosophy has from the very beginning set itself a task which has no competitors – certainly not among scientists. For scientists are not, qua scientists, interested in investigating what the world *is really*. They are happy to accept it as it is. Whether perhaps it is simply illusion, is not a question that bothers them or which they feel a need to entertain. Their job is to describe the phenomenal world – that is, the world as they find it, the world as it appears, and this is a big enough job in itself. To wonder whether as phenomenon it is then somehow at least one remove from something more deeply real, is not of interest to them. But it is of central concern to the philosopher.

There is another way of putting all this which may be even more illuminating. We are all – philosophers, scientists, theologians – concerned with trying to *explain* things. Each of us, however, has a different ideal of explanation – the kind of explanation that will satisfy the scientist will not satisfy the philosopher, and the kind that will satisfy the philosopher may not satisfy the theologian.

For our purposes here suffice it to say that to explain a thing is to try to reduce it into terms which the mind can absorb and accept, which involves, among other things, presenting it in such a way that the mind can accomodate it and come to rest with it. If the mind cannot accomodate or absorb it, then the thing remains a mystery to it – it remains unexplained. For, again, to make a thing intelligible means to process it in such a way that the mind can take it up and absorb it. And this means reducing or translating it into terms endemic to the mind so that in taking it up it will find it acceptable and satisfying – in short, *reasonable*.

Now if this is what, partially at least, is involved in making a thing intelligible to ourselves, then we can begin to see why science can carry us only so far, and why perhaps even philosophy can carry us only so far; that is to say, why science is not enough and why perhaps even philosophy, ultimately, is not enough. Let us consider, for example, the experience of pain, or the phenomenon of sight. Without trying to be either technical or exact, a scientific explanation of pain or sight might take this kind of direction: the reason why, broadly speaking, you feel pain when a pin is stuck into your skin is because the pin separates the fibres of the skin and this produces pain; or in the case of sight, what makes you see things, or have images of things outside the mind are the light rays which strike the object, travel to the retina of the eye and produce there an image of the object. But, we might now ask, are these truly explanations of the phenomena in question? Why should the separation of the fibres of the skin produce pain? What connexion is there between these two? Is there not a mystery here? And similarly with the phenomenon of sight: however intimately these rays of light may enter into the image which is their end product, they are after all only rays of light and not the image, and this will be true regardless what we may in future learn to substitute for the more precise cause here. It will still be impossible for us to see why the two should be connected in this way, and how the one, although different from the other, is yet the same as (or not different from!) it. Yet, of course, from a logical and philosophical point of view, until we are somehow told how this is so, we cannot say we *understand*, although the scientist's work may indeed be finished once he has brought together cause and effect.

This point can be put even more sharply when a more strictly philosophical problem is at stake – say, for example, the problem of evil. Now to try to answer the question why there is evil in the world by noting such things as, perhaps, earthquakes, famine, war, disease, etc., would, of course, be absurd. For in asking such a question, what, of course, we want to know are not the efficient causes of evil (which is all the scientist is interested in, and which we know only too well); rather what we want to know is something else – namely, why there is evil in the world *at all*. We want an explanation which will somehow make evil reasonable (i.e., *acceptable*) to us. To achieve this, it is obviously no use trying to tell ourselves what it is and how it comes to be. Since this is all science can tell us, we are not satisfied with it.

Of course in connexion with such a question it may even be that philosophy too is not enough. For the scientist is interested only in the *how* of things, and this we already know; and the philosopher is interested in the *what* of things, and this too in connexion with this question, we know also; it is only, therefore, the theologian who is interested in the *why* of things, who can answer that question, if indeed there is an answer.

Now the interesting thing here is that the realization that the philosopher's task is somehow radically different from the scientist's arose only slowly and gradually. The struggle has generally been carried on in the area of epistemology and Locke is probably the first philosopher to try to face up to the issues, although he is not always successful in his efforts. Thus it is that we find him remarking in such studies as *Examination of Malebranch* and *Remarks upon Mr. Norris's Books* that no man can tell how ideas are caused and produced in the mind. For motion can produce only motion, and how motion can produce perception is entirely inexplicable. Or as he puts it again in a memorable passage in the former work: Impressions made on the retina by rays of light, I think, he says there, I understand; and motions from there continued to the brain is perhaps something I can perceive; and that these produce ideas in our minds, I am willing to believe – but how all this is accomplished is incomprehensible. It is something, he adds, which we simply must ascribe to God whose ways are past finding out.

But although Locke seems mildly aware that there is a kind of mystery here which science can never hope to unravel, he seems at the same time curiously unable to resist the thought and hope that with the discovery and development of finer instruments it may yet penetrate this mystery and give us such ultimate accounts of the origin of ideas and what lies behind them – a hope which, as he explains, is the reason for his own "extravagant conjectures" concerning such future "experimental" discoveries. And this shows, I think, how far he really still was from seeing the real nature of the problem here. The philosophical developments and insights since Locke, including those of Wittgenstein, have enabled us to see that such hopes are entirely vain, for what stands in our way here are not barriers of a physical sort (which science could learn in time to overcome) but barriers of a logical sort which could never be overcome.

Now although such reflections are indeed already to be found in Locke, it was of course Hume who, in the case of causation, was the first to generalize them and to bring them so clearly before our minds. And it was Kant who was to see this merely as the first step in a whole program whose design was to show how very much a personal thing our knowledge is, and that ultimately what we can know and what we come to know are only ourselves. Now Hume, by undermining, in the way he did, our confidence in causal explanation, made it possible for others who followed not only to adopt a more sophisticated attitude to science and scientific explanation but also a more sophisticated attitude towards philosophy and its own peculiar tasks. Whether this was Hume's intentions here is, of course, irrelevant. The point is rather that other philosophers could not fail to see that if causal explanation fares so badly with such empirical phenomena as sensations and images, then it could hardly fare better with such problems as, for example, the existence of God, immortality, evil, and so on. Here, much more so than with such empirical phenomena as images and sight, the language of causes is hopelessly inadequate.

For some philosophers the language of reasons seemed a possible solution here. But whether these philosophers (Hegel, for example) succeeded in making out their case or not is not something we need to consider here, for whether they succeeded or not, it was this disenchantment with causal explanation that led them to see their own tasks and goals in this new light and gave them renewed confidence to prosecute them in their own ways. There were, after all, it now became very clear, some questions which science was all too obviously unable to answer – most probably because these are questions of an entirely different nature than those it can and has dealt with successfully. This is the point, I think, of Wittgenstein's own comment regarding the "urge towards the mystical." It comes, he says at one point in the *Notebooks*, "of the non-satisfaction of our wishes by science. We *feel* that even if all *possible* scientific questions are answered *our problem is still not touched at all.*"[15]

Philosophical attempts to answer these questions in the way now seen to be demanded by them opened up new and startling insights. Briefly put, it consisted in turning our attention away from the idea of knowledge as being representative and reproductive to seeing it as itself productive and creative. It consisted in turning away from the conception of the mind as a photographic plate registering whatever impinges on it, to regarding it as a kind of self-regulating IBM computer (to use a modern simile) which will respond only to materials prepared and processed for it and which it is specifically designed to absorb. It consisted in seeing that, like the IBM computer, the mind can respond only to that which it can absorb and accomodate, and that therefore unless the materials presented to it have been translated into its terms, properly programmed for it, it will not answer us. The key to our problems therefore were seen to lie in discovering what these terms of reference of the mind are – what it can accomodate and absorb and what it cannot, what it does understand and what it does not, and so on.

A good portion of modern history of philosophy can be read as a search to see just what the mind can, in this sense, come to terms with and accept. Wittgenstein's work belongs to this history. He came to see that the life of the mind being simply language, its dissatisfactions are to be stilled neither by confronting it with causes or reasons but rather, more simply, by clarifying and reordering its language. This is especially the case, he came to see, where philosophical issues are in question. The philosophic "What is ... ?" does not ask, he thus came to see, for a cause or for a reason, but is simply an expression of puzzlement and unclarity. It is to be relieved therefore not by trying to find a cause or a reason but by clarifying its terms, whose confusion initially gave rise to our perplexity.

It is in this sense, I think, that his own thinking on these matters may be regarded as lying, much more so than Existentialism, in the same line of development as that of his predecessors in the history of philosophy. For although Existentialism, in speaking as it often does, of the openness of the future; of our existence in a world in which things simply are without having a sufficient reason for being as they are and

---

[15] Translated by G. E. M. Anscombe. (Oxford: Basil Blackwell, 1961), p. 51.

not otherwise; of our futile attempts to make sense of an essentially senseless world, is not thereby dealing with unrelated matters. However, in dealing with them in this psychological manner, it has tended to lose sight of this over-all direction of modern philosophy. Rather than trying, that is to say, to explore the metaphysical foundations of this condition of ours, it has become absorbed instead in describing the psychological effects which this condition has upon us. Although in doing so it may no doubt in time make a profound contribution to psychology or psychiatry, the same cannot be said of its contributions to the purely philosophical issues here.

For philosophy, as I have tried to show above, has for some time now been absorbed in occupying an area which it has come to recognize as peculiarly and distinctly its own. Although some of the more extreme present-day philosophers call this area Logic, Epistemology is still probably the most appropriate name for it. But whatever it is that we call it, it has for some time now been a subject whose main goal has been to explore the nature of the conceptual systems which we resort to in ordering our experience. What these conceptual systems are? what are their relations to what there is? how do they function? what are their properties? – are the sorts of questions which they have been engaged in exploring. Having come to see the sort of investigation this must be, their exploration has tended to move further and further away from the psychological and more and more in the direction of the purely linguistic or logical.

For, after all, in the real world there is no problem about how it is that Achilles manages to overtake the Tortoise, but there is a problem how he can do it once we begin to *think* about it and conceptualize it. Similarly with the problem of the Freedom of the Will. That we do as a matter of fact feel ourselves to be free, there can be no doubt. But once we begin to *think* about it and wonder how it is possible in view of some of the other things we wish to maintain, we find ourselves in trouble. It is with such "troubles" – "troubles in our thoughts," as Wittgenstein put it – that philosophy has more and more become concerned with. Being conceptual troubles, conceptual puzzles, conceptual paradoxes, conceptual confusions, they are obviously not to be solved by elevated and elevating talk regarding the absurdity of existence and the dark night of the soul. There is absurdity here and there is darkness, but they belong to our conceptual systems and not to existence or the soul.

4

To conclude however:

From one point of view it is possible that Existentialism and Linguistic Philosophy are merely opposite sides of the same coin – one side imprinted with the sign "Absurdity," the other with the sign "Nonsense." Yet from another point of view it is perhaps possible that we have come to a fork in the road – one bearing the sign Psychology, the other, Logic. Linguistic Philosophy has decided to take the road of Logic; Existentialism seems destined and certain to take the road of Psychology. Which of these roads one would be inclined to call the High Road and which the Low, would ordinarily depend upon how the moral theories which issue from their respective epistemological views strike one. Regarding the two theories here in question, there is probably really not very much to choose from. Existentialism does not seem to have one, and the one which issues from Linguistic Philosophy could probably be summed up by paraphrasing Jim Casey's remark in Steinbeck's novel *The Grapes of Wrath* – namely, "There ain't no sin and there ain't no virtue, there's just games people play."

It is no doubt here that Wittgenstein's work is open to its severest and yet perhaps its most illuminating criticism. For if Wittgenstein, and all those who have followed him here, tend to resist the attempt to regard these conceptual systems as ultimate as, for example, Kant believed them to be, they, on the other hand, tend to fall into the opposite error of regarding them as somewhat more arbitrary than our present understanding of them permits us to say. For we may not, it is true, be bound to interpret nature by means of these conceptual schemes, but then nature's response to our varying efforts and the evaluations which we ourselves must therefore place upon them cannot be indifferent to us. Nor can, for that matter, our own needs which also make themselves felt here. And it may well be that it is the diversity of these needs and their conflicting demands – reflected necessarily as they are in our language and playing havoc with it – and not language *itself* as Wittgenstein tended to believe, which mystifies and confuses. Nor are these other demands any less compelling. As William James, whom Wittgenstein greatly admired, and with whom I wish to conclude, put it:

All the magnificent achievements of mathematical and physical science – our doctrines of evolution, of uniformity of law, and the rest – proceed from our indomitable desire to cast the world into a more rational shape in our minds than the shape into which it is thrown there by the crude order of our experience. The world has shown itself, to a great extent, plastic to this demand of ours for rationality. How much farther it will show itself plastic no one can say. Our only means of finding out is to try; and I, for one, feel as free to try conceptions of moral as of mechanical or of logical rationality. If a certain formula for expressing the nature of the world violates my moral demand, I shall feel as free to throw it overboard, or at least to doubt it, as if it disappointed my demand for uniformity of sequence, for example; the one demand being, so far as I can see, quite as subjective and emotional as the other is. The principle of causality, for example – what is it but a postulate, an empty name covering simply a demand that the sequence of events shall some day manifest a deeper kind of belonging of one thing with another than the mere arbitrary juxtaposition which now phenomenally appears? It is as much an altar to an unknown god as the one that Saint Paul found at Athens.[16]

---

[16] "The Dilemma of Determinism," in *Essays in Pragmatism*, ed. by Alburey Castell (New York: Hafner Publishing Co., 1949), pp. 38–9.

NAME INDEX

SUBJECT INDEX